Waldemar Ja

Mourning Cry and

Waldemar Janzen

Mourning Cry and Woe Oracle

Walter de Gruyter · Berlin · New York

1972

Beiheft zur Zeitschrift für die alttestamentliche Wissenschaft

Herausgegeben von Georg Fohrer

125

ISBN 3 11 003848 X

©

1972

by Walter de Gruyter & Co., vormals G. J. Göschen'sche Verlagshandlung — J. Guttentag,
Verlagsbuchhandlung — Georg Reimer — Karl J. Trübner — Veit & Comp., Berlin 30
Printed in Germany
Satz und Druck: Walter de Gruyter & Co.

Dedicated
to my Mother
and
to my Wife

Preface

The present monograph represents, by and large, the second part of the author's doctoral dissertation, which was accepted by the Department of Near Eastern Languages and Literatures of Harvard University in the Spring of 1969. I am grateful to Professors G. Ernest Wright, Frank Moore Cross, Jr., and other members of that Department for their continued interest in and furtherance of my study, and to Professor Georg Fohrer for accepting it into the series of "Beihefte zur Zeitschrift für die alttestamentliche Wissenschaft".

English Scripture quotations have been based on the Revised Standard Version of the Bible, copyrighted 1946 and 1952 by the Division of Christian Education, National Council of Churches of Christ in the U.S.A., and are used by permission. The longer quotation from "The Tale of Aqhat," translated by H. L. Ginsberg in "Ancient Near Eastern Texts" edited by James B. Pritchard, third edition (copyright 1969), is reprinted by permission of Princeton University Press.

December 1971   Waldemar Janzen

Contents

Introduction

The prophetic exclamation *hôy* drew but little scholarly interest prior to the early twentieth century, when its consistent initial position and its formulaic character began to attract the attention of the proponents of the young discipline of form criticism. S. Mowinckel was the first to accord it extensive treatment[1] motivated, to be sure, not by a primary interest in *hôy* as such, but by the need to find a corollary to *'ašrê*, the opening word of the Old Testament beatitudes. This term had confronted him repeatedly in his psalms studies and had been equated by him with the blessing, albeit in "weakened form". Such an equation made it necessary to search for a companion term akin to the curse, a search to which the juxtaposition of beatitudes and woes in Luke 6 20-26 seemed to offer a natural solution. *'Ašrê* and *hôy*, then, were seen by Mowinckel as weakened forms of blessing and curse, parallel in their content and their interrelationship to *bārûk* and *'ārûr*. Their *Sitz im Leben*, he claimed, was the official cultus, from where they found their way secondarily into wisdom literature. Mowinckel set the pattern for many subsequent treatments of *'ašrê* and *hôy*, a pattern traceable through studies such as those of Brun[2], Arvedson[3], Humbert[4], and Keller[5].

A modification of the Mowinckelian characterization of these terms has been introduced by E. Gerstenberger[6]. While preserving the correlation of *hôy* with *'ašrê*, Gerstenberger reverses Mowinckel's thesis as to the sequence of cultus and wisdom in their origin and development. On the basis of themes of popular instruction which he finds in a certain number of *hôy*-oracles he claims the realm of "popular ethos" (*Sippenweisheit/Sippenethos*)[7] as their original *Sitz im Leben* and stresses their didactic function. In pictorial language one might say that the Mowinckelian interpretation of *'ašrê* and *hôy* has been

---

[1] S. Mowinckel, Psalmenstudien V. Segen und Fluch in Israels Kult und Psalmendichtung, 1924.

[2] L. Brun, Segen und Fluch im Urchristentum, 1932.

[3] T. Arvedson, Das Mysterium Christi, 1937, 94—101.

[4] P. Humbert, Problèmes du Livre d'Habacuc, 1944, 18—23.

[5] C. Keller, Les 'Béatitudes' de l'Ancien Testament, in: *Maqqél Shâqédh*, 1960, 88—100.

[6] E. Gerstenberger, The Woe-Oracles of the Prophets, JBL 81 (1962), 249—263.

[7] For a development of this concept, see Gerstenberger's dissertation, Wesen und Herkunft des sogenannten apodiktischen Rechts im Alten Testament, 1965. See also below, 24.

taken like a plant, from roots to shoots, and transplanted from Mo-
winckel's garden plot, cultus, to Gerstenberger's plot, "popular ethos".
This understanding has found explicit approval by H. W. Wolff[8],
Christa Kayatz[9], and others.

In spite of its wide influence the line of interpretation traced so
far has failed to win general acceptance. Many scholars—among them
Hempel, Zimmerli, Gemser, Bertram, Fohrer, Koch, and particularly
H. Schmidt, A. George, C. Westermann, and W. Käser—have gone
their own ways in seeking to understand the termini under discussion,
each rejecting, however, or disregarding the correlation of *'ašrê* with
hôy according to the pattern of blessing and curse, i. e. precisely that
association which provided the impetus and the focal point for the
Mowinckelian interpretation[10].

That this association, appealing as it is, constitutes the Achilles'
heel of Mowinckel's as well as Gerstenberger's thesis becomes evident
when one considers the simple fact that *'ašrê* is extant almost exclusively in the Psalter and in wisdom literature, while *hôy*, with the
exception of I Kings 13 30, is limited to the Prophets. On the other
hand, an association of *hôy* with funerary lamentation—generally
overlooked or brushed aside—is sufficiently clear to warrent an investigation of the relationship of the prophetic *hôy*-words to the
mourning cry.

It is this task which lies before us, after an earlier study of *'ašrê*
has led to an understanding of the origin, meaning and function of
that word totally distinct from any association with *hôy*[11].

---

[8] H. W. Wolff, Amos' geistige Heimat, 1964, 12—23.

[9] Christa Kayatz, Studien zu Proverbien 1—9, 1966, 51f.

[10] A fuller review, with complete bibliographical references, can be found in the writer's
(unpublished) doctoral dissertation, *'Ašrê* and *Hôy* in the Old Testament, Harvard
University, 1969, chapter I.

[11] W. Janzen, A Study of *'Ašrê* in the Old Testament, unpublished ThM thesis, Harvard
Divinity School, 1963. In revised form this thesis constitutes chapter II of the
doctoral dissertation mentioned above. Central aspects of this study are accessible
in the article *'Ašrê* in the Old Testament, HTR 58 (1965), 215—226.

Chapter 1: The Mourning Cry

I. The Problem and the Approach

The provenience and significance of *hôy* in the Old Testament has as yet found no adequate explanation. There can be no doubt that *hôy* is a term associated with lamentation for the dead (I Kings 13 30 Jer 22 18 34 5). In a large number of instances, however, it introduces prophetic announcements of impending calamity. The occasion for the former is death and the funeral, and the mood is mournful. In the latter the occasion is impending punishment, and the mood is frequently one of scorn and bitterness even to the point where the *hôy*-word takes on all the characteristics of a curse (Zech 11 17). In a fair number of passages it is not easily determinable whether the *hôy*-word is a funerary lament (*Totenklage, Leichenlied*) in anticipation of the impending disaster or an invective announcing and/or effecting that disaster.

Merely to distinguish between two (or several) more or less unrelated uses of *hôy* is to capitulate before the problem[1]. It is true that *hôy* is an ejaculated vowel sound of dark timbre and as such occurs in widely separate cultures as a reflex to grief, pain or other emotional release[2]. Nevertheless its circumscribed occurrence and certain fairly stable formulaic features[3] demand the assumption of a basic relatedness of all *hôy*-words, be it through some meaning common to all or through a development from a common origin, a development that would explain the apparent diversity of usage in the extant passages. Studies that want to arrive at an understanding of *hôy* under exclusion of the passages where it is clearly an element in funerary lament are therefore doomed to failure, whether they trace its origin to the curse[4] or to wisdom literature[5]. It is precisely the relationship

---

[1] P. Humbert, Problèmes du Livre d'Habacuc, 19; C. Westermann, Grundformen prophetischer Rede, 1960, 138; E. Gerstenberger, The Woe-Oracles, 250f. In fairness to Westermann and Humbert it must be said that their treatments of *hôy* are marginal to their main concerns.

[2] Hedwig Jahnow, Das hebräische Leichenlied im Rahmen der Völkerdichtung, 1923, 83—87; P. Heinisch, Die Totenklage im Alten Testament, 1931, 22; G. Stählin, κοπετός , . . etc., Theologisches Wörterbuch zum Neuen Testament, III 1938, 837f.

[3] For a discussion of these, see below, 40.

[4] Thus Humbert and Westermann.

[5] Thus Gerstenberger.

between the *hôy* of mourning and the *hôy* of prophetic invective that needs to be illumined.

A firm starting point for our investigation is the fact that at least some *hôy*-words are undisputedly associated with mourning over the dead (I Kings 13 30 Jer 22 18 34 5)[6]. Their exclamation is designated by the verb ספד. They appear in formulae that find counterparts in many mourning rites[7]. That they are at home in these formulae and not coined for the particular instances where they are extant is further confirmed by their slightly inappropriate usage which shows that available standard expressions are involved: A stranger is lamented with *"Hôy, brother!"* (I Kings 13 30); a king with *"Hôy, sister!"* (Jer 22 18)[8]; a boy with *"Hôy, lord!"* (III Kings 12 24m (LXX)). If *hô* is a variant of *hôy*, as is generally assumed, the call to mourning spoken by Amos (5 16-17) is a further witness to *hôy* in funerary lament[9]. This may suffice to point out an indisputable setting in funerary lament for *some hôy*-words in order to gain a firm starting point for an attempt to relate the apparently diverse usages of *hôy* to each other. That the ties between *hôy* and funerary lament are much wider and more subtle, and by no means limited to these obvious instances, will become evident in our next chapter.

If *hôy*, then, at least in a number of indisputable instances, authenticates itself as one of those ubiquitous exclamations of woe that characterize mourning situations throughout the ancient Near East, and beyond it, an attempt to understand it may well begin with an inquiry into the nature and behaviour of such exclamations. We will not expect to find precisely delimitable conceptual connotations or a network of clearly demonstrable etymological interrelationships; the emotive content of these exclamations arises from levels of consciousness much less supervised by rational control and is much more universally human than to be confined to any one language family.

---

[6] The longer LXX text of I Kings 12 24 (III Kings 12 24m) has the prophet Ahijah say about Jerboam's child: καὶ τὸ παιδάριον κόψονται Οὐαὶ κύριε. Regardless of the question of authenticity this is further evidence for the use of such formulae.

[7] Jahnow 86 and 63—67; Stählin 836f.; and the remainder of this chapter.

[8] LXX has only two formulae: "Woe, brother" and "Woe, lord". For our purposes authenticity is less important than the fact that such a combination was considered suitable, whether by prophet or redactor.

[9] This designation is more fitting than the simple "lament"; we must distinguish between this genre and the lament psalms (*Klagepsalmen*). The funerary lament follows upon death, while the lament psalm contains the hope that death may be averted. Cf. H.-J. Kraus, Klagelieder (Threni), 1956, 8; Heinisch, Totenklage, 21. This distinction remains important even when we make allowance for proleptic mourning, a phenomenon widely attested and one with which we will be concerned in connection with *hôy* also. Significantly, *hôy* does not occur in the Psalter.

We will, rather, expect to find a viscous stream, as it were, of more or less undifferentiated emotional content carried by a variety of more or less similar sounds or sound constellations, a stream however, which crystallizes out from time to time into conceptually definable words and formulae[10].

It is unwarranted, on the other hand, to allow the amorphous nature of ejaculated emotive sounds to deter us from the attempt to delineate the dynamics that govern such exclamations and thereby to understand their place within language. A quick glance at some exclamations in modern languages will show that such dynamics exist. In North American English, for example, "Ah!" generally denotes surprise at the unexpected, as well as unexpected recognition. When spoken in a lower key, it can also convey more or less contemptuous rejection of an idea, but it hardly expresses pain. Depending on inflection, "Oh!" might contain regret, acknowledgment, or surprise, but not quite the condescension, rejection, or revulsion that a short "O!" can express[11].

---

[10] This statement is not meant to assign the exclamations in question to a "primitive" level of linguistic development from which, then, "higher" and more complex forms emerge. (For a discussion of theories of the origin of language in simple exclamations, as well as for a forceful critique of such theories, see O. Jespersen, Language, Its Nature, Development and Origin, 1922, 412—442). In fact, no particular theory of the origin of language and the place of our exclamations in it is implicit in our treatment. Instead, we make the much more empirical observation that man at times gives expression to certain experiences, such as mourning and grief, in emotive utterances which lie beyond the realm of communicable conceptual content, while he chooses at other times to communicate these experiences in speech defined by grammatical and lexical convention, speech which can therefore be incorporated into the grammatical parts of speech and fixed in literary genres. These alternatives represent the ends of a continuum, rather than mutually exclusive choices, and it is the place and behaviour of the woe-words along this continuum that forms a part of our investigation.

[11] Our concern here is with the fact of differentation only, a fact that justifies the inquiry into the field of semantic significance of those exclamations that are our subject of study. We are not concerned with their possible psycho-physiological or social origin. (Cf. Jespersen, Language, 414f.). A. Gardiner goes so far as to say of such emotional cries, "This is true speech, and the sound employed is a real word, even if it chance not to be recorded in the dictionary." He continues, "As words or stereotyped units of language, such sounds are called *interjections*, and may be defined as words having reference to given types of psychic reaction and arousing an expectation of use in reference to a particular mood, attitude, or desire presently experienced by the speaker." (The Theory of Speech and Language, 1951[2], 316.) And again, "Though the meaning of words of this class is not less precise than that of other words, it is more complex and less differentiated." (Ibid. 317). The present study shares this view as a working hypothesis, as contrasted with that of Jespersen who would draw a much sharper line between exclamations that are used as interjections

The boundaries of emotive-rational content are largely determined phonetically. This will complicate our investigation into languages no longer spoken and will withdraw certain aspects from access altogether. Considerable information can be gained by an examination of context and setting, however, and it is here that our study will set in.

It is obvious that the evidence from the ancient Near Eastern languages, in particular the Semitic language family, must be examined first. That is not meant to suggest primary interest in etymological relationships, however. Further, it is in an area as the one under discussion where language and time boundaries can and must be transcended, in spite of the very justified cautiousness that has come to prevail in Old Testament studies after so much indiscriminate use of modern Arabic and other extra-Biblical findings. The reasons are twofold: First, ejaculated exclamations are less specifically tied to particular languages than conceptually firmer words, though it is not to be suggested here that they are not culturally determined at all. Even a dog's barking is expressed differently in German and in English(!)[12]. Secondly, the stock of funerary rituals and practices that forms the setting for exclamations of mourning and grief extends with an almost archetypal universality not only throughout the ancient Near East, but through many other ancient and modern cultures.

II. The Mourning Cry in Various Literatures

Akkadian literature provides an exclamatory cry of mourning in the Era-Epic, where Marduk laments the fall of his city Babylon in a sevenfold woe:

> Wehe, Babylon! das ich wie eine Dattelpalme prächtigen
> Ertrag habe tragen lassen: der Wind dörrte ihn
> aus.

only and those that consist of "words from the ordinary language, e. g. *Well! Why! Fiddlesticks! Nonsense!*" (The Philosophy of Grammar, 1965; first published 1924; 90.)

[12] Cf. Jespersen, Language, 415. E. Sapir reminds us of the need to distinguish between conventional interjections and the emotive cries themselves: "The mistake must not be made of identifying our conventional interjections (our oh!, and ah! and sh!) with the instinctive cries themselves. These interjections are merely conventional fixations of the natural sounds. They therefore differ widely in various languages in accordance with the specific phonetic genius of each of these." (Language, 1921, ch. 1). Our study moves on the level of the conventionalized mourning cries, of course, but we need to remain mindful of that universal human experience which finds expression in them.

Wehe, Babylon! das ich wie einen Tannenzapfen mit . . .—
Pollen hatte anfüllen lassen und dessen Fülle ich
nicht genoß.
Wehe, Babylon! das ich wie einen üppigen Garten ange-
legt hatte und dessen Frucht ich nicht aß.
Wehe, Babylon! das ich wie ein Siegel aus elmesu-
Stein an den Hals des Anu gelegt hatte.
Wehe, Babylon! das ich wie die Schicksalstafel in
die Hand genommen hatte und niemand überließ.
(Wehe, Babylon! das . . .)
(Wehe, Babylon! das . . .")[13]

The word translated as *Wehe*, "Woe/Alas" here, and generally, is
u_8-*a* probably to be read $\bar{u}'a$[14]. Its context is clearly that of a funerary
lament, albeit in a highly stylized form of it, as the initial position
and the sevenfold repetition of the "alas" indicate, a form which has

---

[13] P. F. Gössmann, Das Era-Epos, n. d., preface dated Christmas 1955, transliterated
text 29; translation 28. Cf. also A. Pohl, Die Klage Marduks über Babylon im Irra-
Epos, HUCA 23 (1950—51), 405—409, including plate of Tablet IB212, transliteration, and translation.

The date and purpose of the Era-Epic are contested. Pater Gössmann, the editor
of the standard edition, associates the content of the epic with the events leading up
to the destruction of Babylon by the armies of Sennacherib in c. 689 B. C. and
considers a date around 685 B. C. appropriate as the time of composition. (Op. cit.
89f.). W. G. Lambert would date the epic as early as the eleventh century B. C.
(Review of F. Gössmann, Das Era-Epos, Archiv für Orientforschung 18, 395—401).
Gössmann considers the epic to be intended "als ein Amulett, das die bösen Mächte
von Haus und Hof abhalten sollte." (Op. cit. 61). Erica Reiner sees in it an attempt
"to give an etiological explanation for the destruction of Babylon, that is, to explain
under what circumstances and why Marduk was induced to abandon his city and,
as a sequel, how Babylon can be assured that he has now returned there and is
providing once again for the peace and prosperity of his people." (More Fragments of
the Epic of Era. A Review Article, JNES 17, 1958, 42).

[14] Thus W. von Soden, Grundriß der akkadischen Grammatik, 1952, 179, paragraph
124c. Unfortunately neither The Assyrian Dictionary, 1964, nor von Soden's Akkadisches Wörterbuch, 1959—, have progressed to the letter "*u*." Both give some attention to
u_8-*a*, rendered $\bar{u}'a$, under the entry *aja* and *ai II*, respectively. Some scholars render
the u_8-sign as *ù*. Some understand it as '*u-a*. The length of the *u*-sound seems indicated
not only by the exclamatory character of the word, but also by occasional doubling.
The reading *u'ā* has also been suggested. At times the *u*-sound is rendered by *u* or *ù*.
ù'i appears as a variant, just as *ā'i* for standard *aj(j)a*, written *a-a*. Zimmern suggests that the *u*-signs may stand for *ò*. (See below, n. 29.) All of this is evidence not
only for the difficulty of ascertaining the phonetic quality of our exclamation at
such distance, but also for the variations of sound and intonation that will have
characterized the Akkadian woe-cries just as those in more modern languages. (See
the several following footnotes for examples of variant forms and spellings; also the
two dictionaries referred to in this footnote).

developed away, we may assume, from the more common cry "Alas,
brother! Alas, sister!" (I Kings 13 30 Jer 22 18) at an ordinary funeral
and has entered a more sophisticated literary-theological *Sitz im
Leben*. We have not been able to trace *ū'a* or its regular companion
aja to a common funeral context, unless the names *A-a-aḫu-nu* ("Alas,
our brother!"?) and *Ua-a-a-a-ḫa-a-a* ("Alas, our two brothers!"?) give
evidence to it in refracted form[15], yet in the light of the widespread
mourning pattern it seems plausible that such was the background of
this mourning cry[16].

Further evidence for *ū'a*, though not voluminous, shows that this
word was not limited to the realm of mourning, but could be used in a
variety of life situations, as the following passages will indicate. In a
Šurpu-tablet we read:

> . . .
> may his errors be wiped out, his crimes removed,
> his oaths undone,
> his diseases driven away;
> his headache, his restlessness, his gloom, his bad
>   health,
> *woe and lament*[17], sleeplessness, his worry, his
>   gloom, his weariness,
> drive them out today from the body of NN, son of NN[18].

In the Poem of the Righteous Sufferer, Marduk is reported to have
averted a similar catalogue of ills:

> He tore up the root of Impotence like a plant,
> Bad sleep, the pouring out of slumber,
> He took far [away] like smoke with which the
>   heavens get filled.

---

[15] Von Soden understands the names thus. (Akkadisches Wörterbuch, Fascicle I, 23).
J. J. Stamm, on the other hand, translates *A-a-aḫu-nu* as "Wo ist unser Bruder?",
but admits the component "Wehe!" in *Ua-a-a-a-ḫa-a-a*. (Die akkadische Namenge-
bung, 1939, 371 and 163).

[16] A general difficulty besetting our investigations arises from the fact that the un-
sophisticated woe-cries from everyday settings are not, of course, transmitted in
literature unless they happen to stray into a descriptive section of a literary work.
Most of the extant woes have come down to us transplanted into more sophisticated
artistic genres, such as prayers, liturgies or, in the case of the Old Testament, prophetic speech.

[17] The italics are mine, both here and in the following examples.

[18] Erica Reiner, *Šurpu*, AfO, Beiheft 11, 1958, 28 and Table IV, lines 81—86. The
italicized phrase reads *'ù-a a-a-um*. Parallel sources cited have *'u-a-a*. The passage
quoted is an entreaty to Marduk to exercise his power for the benefit of the client
who is not sure as to his offense. (Ibid. 1—3). On the basis of internal evidence the
composition of the *Šurpu*-texts is generally placed into the time between the fifteenth
and the twelfth century B. C.

Woe and Alas, . . .
He drove away like a rain storm . . .[19]

A similar use is evident in a Prayer of the Raising of the Hand to Ishtar:

I am made desolate, and I weep bitterly;
With grief and woe my spirit is distressed.
What have I done, O my god and my goddess?[20]

The context enumerates a long list of further ills: restlessness, sorrow, sighing, bewitchments of body, persecution by enemies, disease, ruin, etc. Similarly a Babylonian penitential psalm:

Gleich Tauben klage ich, von Seufzern sättige ich mich.
Vor *Weh und Ach* ist voll Seufzens sein Gemüt.
Tränen vergießt er, in Klagerufe bricht er aus.[21]

A Marduk—*narû* threatens:

Wer . . . nicht gegeben hat, . . . dieser Fürst, *in Ach und Weh* wird er einhergehen!
Dem König von Babylon und Nippur sind die Länder insgesamt gegeben.[22]

Ashurbanipal prays to Ishtar of Arbela:

Warum muß sich (?) mit böser Krankheit mein Herz
　　vertraut machen (?) (und) ist Verderben in
　　mich gekettet (??) ?
Bedrängniss [sic] im Lande, Unfrieden (?) im
　　Hause weichen nicht von mir;
Irrsal, böse Rede umgiebt mich beständig.
Was schädlich der Seele, was schädlich dem
　　Körper, beugt meine Gestalt.
In Weh und Ach bringe ich meine Tage hin.
Am Tage des Stadtgottes, dem festlichen Tage,
　　bin ich betrübt;
es umfängt mich der Tod, (und) bedrängt (?)
　　(mich)

---

[19] W. G. Lambert, Babylonian Wisdom Literature, 1960, 53. The italicized phrase reads '*ù-ú-a a-a* (Ibid. 52). Lambert dates the Poem of the Righteous Sufferer in the Cassite period. Cf. also ANET 434—437, especially 436, col. II, lines 10—14.

[20] L. W. King, The Seven Tablets of Creation, I 1902, Appendix V, 233, lines 65—67. The italicized phrase reads *ina'-u-a a-a* (232). The prayer comes from the Neo-Babylonian period. Cf. also ANET 383—385, especially 384, col. II, lines 65—67.

[21] H. Zimmern, Babylonische Bußpsalmen, 1885, 10. The italicized phrase reads [ina] *ú'a u á*.

[22] H.-G. Güterbock, Die historische Tradition bei Babyloniern und Hethitern bis 1200, ZA NF 8, (1934), 86. The italicized phrase reads *i-na ú'-i a-a-i* (Ibid. 85). The *narû*-literature is a type of historical fiction or legend in which certain events are told in order to teach a lesson. The Marduk-*narû* under discussion tells a tale of the god himself, rather than a king, as is usual. The excerpt cited is directed against those not heeding the lesson.

> In schmerzlicher Wehklage jammere ich Tag und
>   Nacht;
> ich seufze zu dem Gotte: vergönne (mir), dem
>   Gottlosen, (daß) ich schauen möge dein Licht![23]

We note from this evidence that the word *ū'a* appears in a considerable variety of literary genres other than funerary lament. It is characteristically used as a noun[24] in a chain enumerating various ills, frequently governed by the preposition *ina*. In all instances given *ū'a* is coupled with *aja* in an undulating sequence, like the German *O weh*, though each of the two words can stand alone as well. Thus we read in an Old Babylonian exercise tablet this somewhat enigmatic proverb:

> A man said, '*Alas!*' His boat sank.
> He said, 'Hurrah!' His rudder broke.
> He said, '*Alas!*' and 'Aiaru!' His boat
> came to the side.[25]

For *aja* alone, a Neo-Babylonian letter of an official, *Zêr-ᵈNabû*, gives witness:

Woe concerning the barley! It is destroyed. Speedily go in behalf of it and send the remainder. There is no barley.[26]

The last two instances also show the spontaneous exclamatory quality of these words, while the combination "woe and alas", or something similar, is already a hardened formulaic expression[27].

The haphazard manner in which the formula "woe and alas" is scattered throughout a variety of genres indicates that it does not have

---

[23] C. F. Lehmann, *Šamaššumukîn*, König von Babylonien 668—648 v. Chr., 1892' Part II, 23, Rückseite, lines 3—11. The underlined phrase reads *ina 'u-a ai* (Ibid. 22).

[24] Zimmern thinks differently: "*ôa u â* 'Weh und Ach' fasse ich als Interjektionen = הוֹי und אֲהָהּ , nicht als Nomina (= אוֹי und אַי) [auf]. Auf diese Weise erklärt sich am einfachsten, daß auch in der ‚nicht semitischen' Zeile [of the bilingual penitential psalm cited above, 9, and n. 21] *ôa* und *â* entsprechen — Interjektionen sind eben in allen Sprachen gleich." (Zimmern 116). As to the origin of the words as interjections Zimmern is certainly correct, an origin that remains evident even in nominal usage, but he delimits the parts of speech too sharply, not allowing for fluidity in usage. See above, 5, and n. 11. The application of the delimitation to Hebrew *'ôy* and *hôy* is quite questionable also.

[25] Lambert, Babylonian Wisdom Literature, 274, lines 10—18. The italicized word reads *ú-ua* (translit. KU).

[26] H. F. Lutz, Neo-Babylonian Administrative Documents from Erech, Parts I and II, 1927, 5f., Tablet 2, lines 8—11. The italicized word is *a-a*. Lutz dates the tablet from 625—539 B. C.

[27] The formulaic nature of this cliché is shown not only by the choice of words, but also by their order. Nowhere have I found the order *a-a uₛ-a*.

any particular and defined relationship to these genres, in contrast
to its conscious use in the funerary lament of Marduk.

The content of the formula is generally indicated by the contexts
cited; it stands among statements of sickness, fear, calamity, and other
ills of a personal nature, ills which lead the sufferer to experience life
as sad and burdensome and motivate him to implore the gods for
deliverance. We cannot but note the similarlity of this content to
Old Testament *'ôy*[28, 29] Compare Prov 23 29:

> Who has woe (אוֹי)? Who has sorrow (אֲבוֹי)?
> Who has strife? Who has complaining?
> Who has wounds without cause?
> Who has redness of eye?

Sumerian literature knows a similar exclamation of mourning and
grief, to wit, in the Lament over the Destruction of Ur:

> Its lady cries: '*Alas for my city*,' cries: 'Alas
> for my house;'
> Ningal cries: '*Alas for my city*,' cries: '*Alas for
> my house*.'[30]

Similarly, an instance in The Second Lamentation for Ur:

> Ah, true house, true house;
> ah, its oppressed, its oppressed.[31]

---

[28] For a characterization of what we will call "the *'ôy*-function," see our summary of
Wanke's study, below, 24f.

[29] While etymological relationships between the Akkadian exclamations in question
and their Hebrew formal and functional counterparts must not be overestimated,
in view of the universal character of these words, we note some suggestions. Zimmern
says: "Die Etymologie für *ûa* und *â* liegt sehr nahe. *ûa* ist sicher das assyrische
Äquivalent von hebr. אוֹי , vielleicht geradezu *ôa* statt *ûa* zu lesen. *â* dagegen wird
ebenso hebr. אֲ 'Geheul, wehe!' entsprechen, wie die Negation *â* dem hebr. אַ
Job 22 30." (Zimmern 32). Halévy proposes a different relationship: "L'esprit
doux qui figure au début de *'ua* ou *'uâ* semble indiquer qu'il s'agit, non de l'hèbreu
הוֹי ou אוֹי (Delitzsch) ni de אַ comme je l'ai pensé moimême (Documents religieux
121), mais du וַ araméen (cf. *'aldu* de וְלד) et cela explique la lecture *'ue* que fournit
la glose R V, 40, 4 ef: *u-a(e) = sha ua*, car la contraction de *ai* en *ê* est très fréquente
en assyrien." (J. Halévy, Notes assyriologiques 3, 1888, 334). It is difficult to gain
any certainty here, as one cannot assume that interjections will obey the laws of
linguistic development.

[30] S. N. Kramer, Lamentation over the Destruction of Ur, 1940, 45, lines 245ff. The
italicized phrases read *a urú-mu, a é-mu* (244). Similar exclamations are repeated
throughout for possessions, men, etc. The extant tablets are dated by Kramer to the
period between the fall of the Third Dynasty of Ur and the beginning of Kassite rule
in Babylonia (ANET 455). For further discussion, see T. Jacobsen, American Journal
of Semitic Languages and Literatures 58 (1941), 219—224. Cf. also ANET 455ff.

[31] C. J. Gadd, The Second Lamentation for Ur, Hebrew and Semitic Studies, 1963,
65, line 60. The Sumerian reads: *a é-zi é-zi a šaga-bi šaga-bi*. The occasion for the

From the Curse over Akkade we hear:

> Die alten Frauen hören nicht auf (mit dem Schrei)
> 'ach, meine Stadt'
> die alten Männer hören [ni]cht auf (mit dem Schrei)
> 'ach, ihre Mensch[en],'
> die Kultsänger hören [ni]cht auf (mit dem Schrei)
> 'ach, das Ekur' . . .[32]

In the lamentations over Tammuz lengthy mourning chains are introduced in the same manner:

> Alas   my hero Damu.
> Alas   child, lord Gišzida.
> Alas   god of the tender voice and shining eyes.
> Alas   Lamga, lord of the net.
> Alas   prince lord of invocation.
> Alas   my heavenly wailer.
> The raging storm has brought him low
> . . . .
> His mother wailing   let her begin wailing for him[33].

In every case the sign "A" renders the interjection of woe. Von Soden considers it the equivalent of Akkadian "a(-a)."[34] Landsberger posits a phonemic distinction between Sumerian "A" in ordinary usage, as in the word for "water," and "A" used as an exclamation of woe. He suggests the possibility that the latter may have been pronounced as a drawn-out, open "e" ("ein langgedehntes offenes e")[35·36].

---

poem is the destruction of Ur by the Elamites, just as for the (First) Lamentation over the Destruction of Ur.

[32] A. Falkenstein, Fluch über Akkade, ZA NF 23, (1965), 72. The Sumerian reads:

> *a urú-mu*
> *a lú-u [lù^{lu}]-bi*
> *a é-kur*

Narāmsîn had incurred guilt against the Ekur of Enlil in Nippur. Enlil called the Guti and gave all of Babylonia into their hands. Thereupon eight of the chief gods attempted to placate Enlil by cursing Akkad, the city of Narāmsîn. The text concludes with the description of the realization of the curse (Ibid. 46). Falkenstein dates the composition to the time of the Third Dynasty of Ur (Ibid. 50).

[33] S. Langdon, Sumerian and Babylonian Psalms, 1909, 313.

[34] Akkadisches Wörterbuch, Lieferung 1, 23, entry "ai II." Further Sumerian occurrences are given there, as well as in The Assyrian Dictionary, I, entry "aja."

[35] B. Landsberger, Materialien zum sumerischen Lexicon, 1951, II: Die Serie Ur-e-a = nâqu, 29f. and 126.

[36] The sign u_8 is also found in Sumerian as the equivalent to Akkadian *û'a*, for example, P. Haupt, Akkadische und sumerische Keilschrifttexte, 1881, 116, No. 14; transliteration and translation in Zimmern 10, lines 11/12. On the basis of the etymology

We note that again a short interjection is used both as a mourning cry and as a marker of inner pain generally. In our first three citations it appears as the spontaneous outcry of people confronted with grief and suffering, while the lament for Tammuz shows it embedded consciously into an artistic composition.

In Ugaritic, the exclamation of special interest to us is y. In most of its occurrences it is the standard vocative particle and appears in combinations such as $yšpš$ ("O Sun"), ybn ("O son"), $yilm$ ("O gods"), etc.[37]. There is one passage, however, that uses this particle in the context of lamentation over the dead. This passage will require our detailed attention below[38] and will, therefore, not be discussed further here. At this point we note the fluidity between a vocative particle and a cry of woe. That the particle in question is y is interesting also, in view of Arabic $yâ$ and Aramaic $yî$[39].

In Arabic the most frequent interjection of mourning is $yâ$, but it is interchanged or combined with a variety of others: wa, ah, $ahaih$, $haih$, $wēli$, depending at times, perhaps, on the region, but frequently employed in conscious variation or cumulative effect:

> *məazzîje: ah ja-ḫûja jalli ma freḫtiš bik*
> Eine Kondolierende: *Ach*, mein Bruder,
> daß ich mich über dich nicht freuen
> konnte![40]

> *ahaih ʿalêh . . . ahaih maḍrûb . . . ahaih
> ja ʿarîs . . . ʿarûṣa ja ʿarûṣa . . .*
> *Weh* über ihn . . . *Weh* über den
> plötzlich Gestorbenen . . . Wehe dem
> Bräutigam . . . du Braut, *o* du Braut . . .[41]

---

suggested by him (see above, 11, n. 29), Zimmern sees this as an intrusion from the Semitic realm and gives two options: "Da *ûa* sich als gut semitisches Wort gibt, so bleibt die Wahl, entweder anzunehmen, daß der Lautwert '*u* des Zeichens semitischen Ursprungs, im Sumerischen deshalb das Ideogr. mit einem andern Lautwerte zu lesen sei, oder dem Ideogramm die Bedeutung 'Seufzen' für das Rein-Sumerische überhaupt abzusprechen und mit der Lesung *u-a* für eine blose [sic] Eintragung aus dem Assyrischen in das Sumerische zu halten, wobei der Lautwert '*u* ganz gut sumerischen Ursprungs sein, und gerade wegen seines Gleichklangs mit ass. *û* 'Seufzer' den Grund zu der misbräuchlichen [sic] Ideogrammverwendung abgegeben haben kann. Ich entscheide mich für letztere Annahme" (Op. cit. 32).

[37] C. H. Gordon, Ugaritic Textbook, 1965, Glossary, 407, entry 1060; and G. D. Young, Concordance of Ugaritic, 1956, 31, entry 783.

[38] See below, 27ff.

[39] See below, 14 and 29; n. 98.

[40] P. Kahle, Die Totenklage im heutigen Ägypten, in: H. Schmidt, Eucharisterion, I 1923, 363. My italicizing of the words of interest to us in this and the following citations.

[41] Ibid. 367.

> *Jâ ṛabra' ḳamarki ṛâb jâ wêli*
> *jâ laǧǧa ḥarîmo tîka-l-lêli*
> *jâ laǧǧa ḥarîmo bahhatat ḥêlî*

> O du mit Staub Bestreute, dein Mond
>   ist untergegangen — — o wehe!
> o Geschrei seiner Frauen in jener Nacht,
> o Geschrei seiner Frauen, es verdarb
>   mein Wohlbefinden . . .[42]

As Ugaritic *y* Arabic *yâ* is, first of all, the commonly used vocative particle, quite outisde of any context of lamentation. When it enters the realm of mourning, *yâ* at times clearly preserves its ordinary vocative function:

> *Jâ dâfiʿ ilbela*
> *bâṭil ʿannak*
> *welâhu min ṣaḥîḥ*

> O du, der entfernt das Unheil,
>   es gilt nicht für dich,
>   es ist ja nicht wahr![43]

The mourning cry can appear as a simple address, without a following statement, as in the ever-repeated "O my brother! O my sister!"[44] Once associated with lamentation, it can be transferred to other parties, factors, or objects somehow connected with the deceased. A veritable catalogue is found in Kahle's collection:

> Die Kondolierenden schreien mit lauter
> Stimme, und eine sagt: [o] meine
> Schwester! und die andere [o] mein Bruder!
> die Leidtragende: O Tag von Schwärze, o
> mein Ruin, o Schließung meiner
> Tür, o mein Löwe, o mein Kamel,
> o Vater der Waisen, wem hast du sie hin-
> terlassen nach dir, o mein Schwindel, o
> mein Abgeschnittensein, o meine Bedürftigkeit
> nachdem du fort bist![45]

This typology is suggested as offering a descriptive account of the apparent continuity of vocative *yâ* and the *yâ* of lamentation. Historical development through these phases is not necessarily implied. A similar pattern might be posited for Ugaritic and, as we shall see, for Egyptian and Greek lamentation as well.

---

[42] A. Musil, Arabia Petraea, III 1908, 432f.
[43] G. H. Dalman, Palästinischer Diwan, 1901, 324.
[44] For example, Kahle 357, but also throughout the literature.
[45] Ibid. 357; "meine Schwester" and "mein Bruder" are preceded by *yâ* in the original, though Kahle does not translate o.

The development of these simple exclamations into sophisticated literary genres has been traced by Goldziher in an extensive study[46]. He summarizes:

> Aus den Saǧ'-Rufen werden zunächst kurze metrische Sprüche von wenigen Zeilen, zuweilen auch längere Reǧez-Lieder, aus denen sich dann stufenweise die ausgebildete Marṯija in der metrischen Mannigfaltigkeit und Kunstform der Ḳaṣîden-Gedichte entwickelt. Dasselbe gilt auch vom musikalischen Element der Todtenklage. Die einfachen volksthümlichen Melodien der Klagefrauen werden durch Gesangskünstler zum Trauergesang entwickelt . . .[47]

We note also that in Arabic just as in Akkadian, words characteristically associated with death and funeral can also be used in bemoaning some other calamity experienced, i. e. in what we might call the "ôy-capacity." Here, for example, with reference to hopeless love:

> Eine Schöne bei den Kurden — —
> o weh mir, schwarz sind ihre Augen!
> ich bot meine Seele dar und die Stute,
> nicht glaube ich, sie geben sie mir.[48]

To etymologize concerning the interjections discussed seems fruitless. The general sound quality of interjections of mourning will be treated briefly below[49].

The Egyptian funerary laments, gathered in considerable number by Lüddeckens[50], seem at first to diverge somewhat from the pattern observed so far. Instead of the wailing and disconsolate despair that characterizes death throughout the ancient Near East and the Arabic world, we are confronted with beautifully composed hymns that congratulate the deceased upon the privilege of entering the "West":

> a) Zum Westen,
> zum Westen,
> zum Ort, wo Deine Sehnsucht weilt!

> b) Worte zu sagen seitens der Leute von
> Pe, der Leute von Dep, der Leute
> von Busiris,
> der Leute von Unu, der Leute vom 'Hause
> der grossen Rinder':

---

[46] I. Goldziher, Bemerkungen zur arabischen Trauerpoesie, Wiener Zeitschrift für die Kunde des Morgenlandes 16 (1902), 307—339. For a similar development in Egyptian, see Erich Lüddeckens, Untersuchungen über religiösen Gehalt, Sprache und Form der ägyptischen Totenklagen, 1943, 175.

[47] Goldziher 308.

[48] Dalman 352. Cf. also 330. The o weh [my italics, W. J.] is jâ wêli in both examples; cf. Hebrew אוי לי.

[49] See below, 29, n. 98.

[50] Lüddeckens op. cit.

Willkommen im Westen!
Ooh! Du [mit Gesundheit ?] Beschenkter!
Du bist nicht dahingegangen tot;
Du bist dahingegangen lebend,
(damit) Du setzest Dich auf den Thron des
                    Osiris,
indem Dein ... Szepter in Deiner Hand war,
als Du dem Lebenden befahlst.[51]

The funerary practices, however, often preserved graphically[52],
show many of the characteristic accoutrements of mourning known
from the ancient Near East, such as wailing women, tearing of hair,
beating of breasts, pouring of dust onto the head, rending of gar-
ments, sitting in dust[53]. It becomes clear that the texts represent
formal liturgies expressing official theology and reformulating the
deeply human experience of death as an enemy into glorious hope[54].

It does not surprise, then, to find some texts in which a gloomy
pessimism breaks through:

Worte zu sagen seitens der Klagefrauen:
Wehe! Wehe!
Heil! heil! heil! heil!
Klaget unermüdlich!
Ach, der Verlust!

Der gute Hirte
    ist gegangen zum Lande der Ewigkeit, ...

Der Du reich an Leuten (warst),
    Du bist im Lande, das die Einsamkeit liebt,

Der es liebte, seine Beine zu öffnen zum Gehen,
    ist gefesselt, eingewickelt und gehemmt!

Der, reich an Stoffen, sich zu kleiden liebte,
    schläft im abgelegten Kleid von gestern![55]

---

[51] Ibid. 29.

[52] Ibid. 18. 111. 123. 126.

[53] Ibid. 2—16.

[54] We have here an early instance of the tendency of the great religions as well as the
advanced legal codifications to suppress, or at least limit, the mourning rites under
discussion, a tendency that seems to have been invariably unsuccessful. Both
Christianity and Islam tried unsuccessfully to eradicate these rites. (Maria Cramer,
Die Totenklage bei den Kopten, 1941, 77. 78f. 82f. 85f. 92. 95; Goldziher 321—323.
334). Solon restricted such practices sharply (Cramer 94) and the Roman Law of
Twelve Tablets (451 B. C.) forbade them (ibid.). Rabbinic Judaism controlled them
by defining their application precisely. (H. L. Strack and P. Billerbeck, Kommentar
zum Neuen Testament aus Talmud und Midrasch, IV 1956, Part 1, 578—592:
"Bestattung der Toten.")

[55] Lüddeckens 112. Cf. 134. 135 for similarly pessimistic texts. See also Lüddeckens'
discussion 171f. The tension between jubilation and despair is brought out in an-

Again we observe that the common vocative particle i[56] has a prominent place in funerary lament. Lüddeckens says: "Sie [die Toten-klage des Alten Reiches] besteht in der Hauptsache nur in kurzem Anrufen des Verstorbenen, und die Interjektion gehört zum Anruf."[57] It is varied with other interjections, however[58]. The drafting of the vocative interjection into the service of lamentation (and of jubila-tion!) is beautifully illustrated by an orthographic development:

> Der nahezu gleiche Zeichenbestand von *ihj Jubel* und *ihj Klageruf* weist darauf hin, daß beide Worte zurückgehen auf *eine* (lautmalende) Wiedergabe erregten Rufens — sei es aus Lust oder Schmerz —, die auch der Interjektion *ihj* zugrunde liegt, . . . Diese wird in den Sargtexten (Coffin-Texts I 239d) als Äußerung sowohl des Jubels als auch des Schmerzes genannt:
>
> [Hieroglyphic text]
> *Ooh, ooh, ooh, ooh! (zu rufen) seitens des*
> *Frohlockenden und seitens des Klagenden*[59].

Lüddeckens posits a development from the simple mournful cry addressing the deceased to the more complex forms, a development similar to that suggested above in connection with our discussion of the situation in Arabic[60, 61].

The Greek antiquity, from earliest records on, shows funerary and mourning rites almost identical with those of the Near East and possibly borrowed from it[62], and here also it can be said:

> Der Hauptausdruck des spontanen wie des berufsmäßigen κοπετός waren wohl formlose Klagerufe, die jedoch die Vorläufer der geformten θρῆνοι waren.[63]

Such a cry of lament is, again, the common vocative "ὤ" which is written "ὦ" when used as a vocative, and "ὤ" when used as an

---

other poem, 159; in the lament cited by us it is intimated in the introjected fourfold "Hail!".

[56] Ibid. 17.   [57] Ibid.

[58] Ibid. 27f.

[59] Ibid. 27. Hieroglyphic orthography adds an additional sign to *ihj* (mourning) to arrive at *ihj* (jubilation).

[60] See above, 14f.

[61] Lüddeckens describes the development as follows: "Im AR besteht die Klage . . . aus kurzen klagenden Anrufen an den Toten . . . Auch sie haben wir uns sicher wiederholt gerufen zu denken . . . Es ist das wohl die einfachste Art der Klage, bestehend in fortwährendem Ausstoßen solcher Anrufe an den Verstorbenen. Die Anfügung eines kurzen Satzes . . . ist schon ein kleiner Schritt zur größeren Aus-führlichkeit der uns aus dem NR erhaltenen Klagen. Neben ihnen waren aber zweifellos zu allen Zeiten die anspruchslosen Rufe an den Toten beim Begräbnis zu hören" (ibid. 175).

[62] Stählin 832ff. 837.

[63] Ibid. 837.

exclamation of surprise, joy and pain. It is varied with a great variety of other interjections, however: ἰώ, ἰὼ μοί, ἰωά, οἴ, οἰοῖ, οἴμοι, οἴμμοι, οἴ γώ, ὤμοι, ἔ, αἰαῖ. Their variation and interchange will be illustrated by excerpts from Oedipus at Colonus:

Oedipus:
ὤμοι ἐγώ, τί πάθω, τέκνον ἐμόν;
. . . .
Chorus:
ἰὼ ὢ ὤ
Oedipus:
δύσμορος
Chorus:
ὢ ὤ
Chorus:
ὢ Ζεῦ
. . . .
Chorus:
ἰώ
Oedipus:
ἰὼ δῆτα μυρίων γ' επιστροφαὶ κακῶν[64].

Biblical οὐαί does not occur outside of the LXX and the New Testament, however, though LXX varies it with ὤ. We note again the use of the vocative particle in mourning, the variation of exclamatory particles, and the combination of the *hôy*-function with the '*ôy*-function in the same interjection, as the formations ὤμοι and οἴμοι show clearly (cf. אוי לי).

The boundaries for that complex of mourning rites and formulae described so far could be extended to embrace cultures and languages less closely associated with those considered, a fact which shows that we are working on a bed-rock level of human feeling, behaviour, and linguistic expression. The evidence treated so far seems sufficient, however, to establish a model for the behaviour of certain interjections, a model that will, it is hoped, offer an understanding of the relationship of '*ôy*, funerary *hôy* and exclamatory *hôy*, which has sufficient intrinsic plausibility to be illuminating and clarifying. Only after that has been accomplished will it be possible to inquire into the relationship of prophetic invective *hôy* to this complex of interjections.

The model may be compared to a triangle consisting of the vocative particle (*Anruf*), the mourning cry (*Klageruf*) and the cry of terror and self-pity (*Schreck- und Angstruf*). The transition of the *Anruf* into the *Klageruf* has been seen to be a well-attested and intrinsically understandable phenomenon. This development is not unilinear, how-

---

[64] Oedipus at Colonus, lines 215. 226—228. 33—37, in Sophocles, I 1912 (with an English translation by F. Storr), in the Loeb Classical Series.

ever; the particle in question continues to function as *Anruf* (and may diversify into other directions as well, such as that of *Jubelruf*), so that it is almost indeterminable in many contexts whether the deceased person is addressed or lamented. At times a slight phonetic (and/or orthographic) variation may enter in.

We have observed, further, that the *Klageruf*, whether also extant as *Anruf* or not, almost always functions as *Schreckruf* as well. A clear distinction between exclamations lamenting the dead and those bemoaning one's own or others' threatening, terrifying, or hopeless situation can seldom be drawn. Especially in the mourning context the mourner embraces the total situation into his wailing, as he moves from "Alas for you!" to "Woe is me!" with natural ease.

Thirdly, there is the tendency for the *Klageruf* to seek variations. It has been suggested that mourning laments were composed spontaneously[65]. One might also ascribe the variation to mental agitation: just as an agitated state, be it excitement or pain, tends to express itself in tossing to and fro or walking up and down, its vocal expression undulates from cry to cry. The companion word of the *Klageruf* may be phonetically close, or create an antiphonal effect, or simply present a variation. Some *Klagerufe* may be primitive sounds (*Urlaute*), like the sound of sighing, but the variety of *Klagerufe* points also to some culturally determined conditioning. In sophisticated usage these variants may be repeated rhythmically, or antiphonally, or in some other artistic arrangement. They may harden into formulae, such as u_8-*a* (*u*) *a-a*[66]. Eventually they become more or less firmly embedded in more complex literary creations.

Conceptually these exclamations can hardly be defined. They are the markers for certain existentially or emotionally experienced situations. At times, however, they crystallize into words of more or less clear rational connotation and grammatical definability, so that they can fulfill grammatical functions, as the noun u_8-*a* in the Akkadian enumerations of calamities.

III. The *Hôy* of Mourning in Relation to Vocative *Hôy* and to '*ôy*

With this model in mind we need to reconsider the evidence for the relationships among the various types of *hôy*, and between these and '*ôy*. Interpreters have generally grouped the *hôy*-words into three classes: (1) those belonging to funerary lament, (2) those constituting vocative appeal/address (*Aufruf*, *Anruf*), and (3) those expressing

---

[65] Lüddeckens 175 and 177 (*Stegreifdichtung*).
[66] Cf. German *O weh!* or *Weh und Ach*.

prophetic indictments[67]. They have, as a rule, brushed aside (1) and (2) in order to devote their attention to (3). Wanke is characteristic here:

> Ein auf den ersten Blick uneinheitlicheres Bild [als אוֹי] bietet das Wörtchen הוֹי mit seinen verschiedenen Bedeutungsnuancen, da es zunächst drei voneinander unabhängig scheinenden Bereichen zuzuordnen ist. *Zwei davon geben keine weiteren Probleme auf.* [My italics. W. J.] In I Reg 13 30 Jer 22 18 34 5 Am 5 16 (הוֹ) ist הוֹי der Ruf der Totenklage, der in den meisten Fällen mit einem Substantiv das Verhältnis des Klagenden zu dem Toten beschreibt. Als einen auffordernden Ruf, der etwa mit 'ha!', 'los!' oder 'auf!' zu übersetzen wäre, wird man das in Jes 1 24 17 12 18 1 55 1 Jer 47 6 Sach 2 10f. zu verstehen haben.[68]

In the light of the results of this chapter such demarcations seem unhappy. We have seen that appellation and lamentation merge in the simplest mourning formula, "Oh/alas, brother/sister/lord!" We are not surprised, then, to find the woe of funerary lament in contexts that shade over into what can be called *Anrufe/Aufrufe*, even though these never lose that sombre quality which has, perhaps, been the cause for the employment of *hôy* in funerary contexts and which has certainly been nourished by that context[69]. The Hebrew language does not, of course, form a vocative by the use of a particle, and yet the use of *hôy* does underscore the invoking (*anrufende*) quality of the words following. Such instances are Is 18 1 55 1 and Jer 47 6. For Is 1 24 a funerary context will be argued below[70], while the three *hôy*-words of Zech 2 10f. simply lack any clear relationship to their present context.

The point to be emphasized here, however, is the fact that these *Anrufe/Aufrufe* do not constitute a different and special type of *hôy*, but share in a quality very characteristic of the funerary *hôy*, and that the latter itself shares in this appellative quality[71].

---

[67] Westermann 138. Humbert 19. Also, with some modification, Gerstenberger, The Woe-Oracles, 250f. G. Wanke, אוֹי und הוֹי, ZAW 78 (1966), 217. Cf. also BDB and KB.

[68] Wanke loc. cit.

[69] A possible exception may be Is 55 1. There *hôy* seems to be no more than a call to attention. In contrast to all other instances it is followed by an exuberant invitation to life. In view of the transformation of forms so characteristic of II Isaiah one might raise the question, however, whether we are not dealing with a deliberately chosen death-life contrast here. Most of the major Greek witnesses as well as the Vulgate omit the *hôy;* MT, 1Q Isaiah a, and Codex Ephraemi have it. We consider the omission as a smoothing out due to the unusual usage ond consider the *lectio difficilior* original.

[70] See below, 57f.

[71] It is even less necessary to think of homonyms, unless one considers all interjections of similar sound homonyms, as they can rarely be related to each other etymologically with any degree of certainty.

We wish to argue, further, that this invoking, appellative quality is an ingredient of the "prophetic *hôy*-words"[72] as well, contrary to the assertion of Gerstenberger that "The normal prophetic woe-form contains general and timeless indictments of historically unspecified evildoers"[73], unless, of course, one makes the evidence for direct address the principle of selection by which to exclude certain *hôy*-words from the "normal prophetic woe-form"[74].

We start with the generally accepted recognition that *hôy* is not at home in its present prophetic context, but has been introduced into it from another realm. To peel out an original formula from its secondary prophetic context is difficult, although there is far-reaching agreement that its kernel is the word *hôy* itself, followed by the designation of its addressee, usually in the form of a participle which characterizes him. This designation can then be expanded by parallel cola or bi-cola and eventually shades over into the expected forms of the prophetic judgement speech[75].

A methodological question arises at this point: How far does one "peel" to free an "original" *hôy*-formula? Ultimately, as we have seen, it is the interjection itself which constitutes the basic cry of lamentation and therefore the smallest formal cell, and indeed we have such one-word *hôy*-formulae[76]. And yet the immediate context, though not perfectly stable formulaically, is generally drawn into the discussion of *hôy*, and rightly so. Gerstenberger draws the line in such a way as to exclude any direct address in the second person. He claims that "in the 'woe-threat combination' [of the "prophetic woes"] the personal style in the latter part contradicts the impersonal attitude of the former element"[77].

---

[72] Even though all *hôy*-words occur in the Prophets, except I Kings 13 30 (where it is also spoken by a prophet), we will for convenience's sake, reserve the term "prophetic *hôy*/woe" for the third group in the traditional classification (see above, 19f.).   [73] Gerstenberger, The Woe-Oracles, 252.

[74] This is the tendency of Gerstenberger (ibid. 251ff.), a methodological error that cannot but vitiate his conclusions. Of course, we are not arguing that there are *no* impersonal *hôy*-words, but merely, that *hôy* must not be tied to impersonal speech, just as *'ašrê* can be spoken impersonally, as well as followed by a pronominal suffix of the second person, or by a proper noun. Funerary lament characteristically alternates between addressing the dead directly and speaking about him in the third person. In the revenge-context, which will be suggested for certain *hôy*-words below, such a fluctuation between direct and indirect address becomes quite understandable also.

[75] Cf. Westermann 138; Gerstenberger, The Woe-Oracles, 250—254; Wolff, Amos' geistige Heimat, 1964, 14; Humbert 20f.

[76] Is 17 12 Jer 30 7 Zech 2 10 (2×).

[77] Gerstenberger, The Woe-Oracles, 253. The passages referred to are Is 5 9. 13f. 24 28 2-4 30 3-5 31 2-3 Mic 2 3 Hab 2 16 Zeph 3 5.

If that "personal style in the latter part" proves to follow the
"impersonal" formula in the larger number of instances[78], however,
it is good form-critical method to ask whether there is not at least
a formal affinity between the woe-formula in its narrow sense and
personal address. Could adoption of the *hôy*-formula by the prophets
not be a result, among other factors, of the fact that it was germaine
to the personal, addressee-directed speech of the prophet?

The impression that this is so is strengthened by the existence of
some formulae that lock the *hôy* and the personal address into indissoluble literary units:

> Woe to you, destroyer, who yourself have
>   not been destroyed;
> you treacherous one, with whom none has
>   dealt treacherously;
> When you have ceased to destroy, you will
>   be destroyed;
> and when you have made an end of dealing
>   treacherously,
>   you will be dealt with treacherously.
>
> (Is 33 1)

Of course, one can say that "*hôy*, destroyer" is an originally self-
contained formula, expanded secondarily by the prophet. One has to
grant, even then, however, that the "expansion" was not a haphazard
throwing together of unequal elements, but a consciously constructed
work of literary art for which the artist carefully selected building
bricks that fitted together. Contextual evidence, then, makes it highly
plausible that the prophetic woes — participial constructions notwith-
standing — share with the *hôy*-words which clearly belong to mourning or appellation a common affinity for the realm of direct and
personal communication. Only by stubborn insistence on a categorical
distinction between the various *hôy*-groups and on the radical independence of the *hôy*-formula — understood as a smallest literary
unit — from contexts into which it must then have been inappro-
priately incorporated, can one set the prophetic woes apart as charac-

---

[78] A survey of all *hôy*-passages results in the following picture: In 31 pericopes the
immediate context of *hôy* shows evidence that a specific addressee is in view: a
question or command in the second person, a finite clause addressing a second person,
or simply a noun designating the one addressed. In 5 pericopes the woe-formula
stands contextless. In 11 pericopes impersonal third-person speech does not flow over
into personal address. Even if one subtracts the clear instances of funerary usage and
the *hôy*-words that constitute an appeal *(Aufruf/Anruf)* from the first category,
— a methodology that we have already rejected as arbitrary — the remaining prophetic woes also could in no way be characterized as belonging to general and impersonal speech.

teristically belonging to the realm of impersonal pronouncement of general truths.

But we ask even beyond contextual evidence, whether it is really necessary to understand the participle, so frequently following upon *hôy*, as the hallmark of such impersonal pronouncement of general truths. The very fact that the place after *hôy*, often occupied by a participle, can be filled by a proper noun or precise designation of a particular addressee (Is 10 5 29 1 Ez 34 2 Nah 3 1 Zeph 2 5 Zech 2 11, etc.) suggests that the less specifically delimiting participle may also be understood as designating a specific addressee rather than a general category, a "you who . . ." rather than "he who . . .", at least in some passages. This possibility is vividly illustrated by a passage like Amos 4 1-2 — not a *hôy*-pericope — where a direct address to a specific addressee (verse 1a) is expanded by a parallel bi-colon further designating the addressee by three participial phrases (verse 1b)[79]. Participial construction as such, then, cannot be adduced as evidence that "the normal prophetic woe-form contains general and timeless indictments of historically unspecified evildoers."[80] On the contrary, it is very likely that at least some of the participles following upon *hôy* are intended as vocatives in a life context of direct confrontation[81].

---

[79] Wolff cites this word as an example of a special type of prophetic motivation *(Begründung)*. He notes the frequency of the participial expansion of the motivating address and adds: „Die besondere Eigentümlichkeit dieser Form ist die Wendung in das 'Persönliche'." (H. W. Wolff, Die Begründung der prophetischen Heils- und Unheilssprüche, ZAW 52, 1934, 4).

   Post-Biblical use of the participle as a veritable form of address, terse and self-contained, is given by T. Canaan: "Every one of these verbs [to curse, put to shame, disgrace, etc.] may be used in the simple form of *'ism el-mf'ūl*, 'passive participle,' . . . . Insults connected with sexual life where the insulted plays a passive part as well as insults directed against health are also used in this form . . . . Most of the other insults, especially those connected with impurity, have the form of the active principle [sic.; should be "participle"] or noun of agent *('ism el-fā'il)*: qawwād, 'akūt, fādjir." (The Curse in Palestinian Folklore, JPOS 15, 1935, 259). Such participial curses are frequently preceded by vocative *yâ* (ibid. 256f.).

[80] Gerstenberger, The Woe-Oracles, 252.

[81] E. Kautzsch (ed.), Gesenius' Hebrew Grammar, par. 116s., allows this in principle and even provides some (textually not completely certain) examples where an expected personal pronoun of the second person must be understood as the subject, even though it is omitted, as is frequent for a personal pronoun subject of a participial clause. We take the use of the article with a number of participles following *hôy* (Is 5 20 10 1 29 15 31 1 Am 5 18 6 1 Hab 2 6) to be vocative in nature (cf. ibid. par. 126e), thus supporting our argumentation further.

Excursus: Popular Ethos

This conclusion in itself does not deny a relationship of *hôy* to the realm of popular ethos (*Sippenethos, Sippenweisheit*); the *'ašrê*-formula which frequently employs a participle and to which much of our discussion therefore applies also, is certainly prominent in wisdom speech[82]. Our critique of Gerstenberger's theory concerning the origin of *hôy* in popular ethos arises from certain considerations with respect to the origin and definition of literary forms. The people, the "folk", will, in their everyday endeavors, speak about every aspect of life: worship, agriculture, death and funerals, government, laws, sickness, etc. In that sense every specialized literature could be traced to a sub-stratum of "folk-lore": folk-law, folk-medicine, folk-worship, etc., including folk-wisdom. How the latter may have been operative and may have become the source of incipient wisdom forms has been shown by Ludwig Köhler in his discussion of the *sôd*[83]. This realm of speech is characterized by a degree of shapelessness, "formlessness" in the literal sense; its concerns gain form, become literarily distinctive forms of speech, only as the specialist takes them up and perfects them as the language of his domain: they become laws, liturgies, incantations, sagas, wisdom teachings, etc. To say with Gerstenberger that the woes ultimately derive from popular ethos need not be denied; of course the "folk" said "*hôy!*" here and there. The more significant question is, however, whether *hôy* became a distinctive term or formula in a distinctive realm where it acquired a certain predictability of occurrence and function. For *'ašrê* this happened in the wisdom context, understood in the stricter sense of that term, even though not exclusively there. For *hôy*, on the other hand, the road from popular use to its Biblical employment by the prophets does not lead through wisdom literature with its didactic interests, but through funerary lament with its distinctive complex of emotional manifestations.

We proceed to a re-examination of the relationship between the *hôy*-words, now seen as tied together by a dynamic made understandable through a study of the behaviour of certain exclamatory interjections, to its companion word, *'ôy*. The similarity and diversity between *hôy* and *'ôy* have been noted here and there, but have generally been accorded slight attention, each scholar treating the two as synonymous or as different, depending on personal viewpoint or interest.

G. Wanke[84], stimulated by the indiscriminate treatment of the two by Gerstenberger and Wolff, has presented a careful analysis of

---

[82] Cf. W. Janzen, *'Ašrê* in the Old Testament, op. cit.
[83] Der hebräische Mensch, 1953, 88—94.   [84] Wanke op. cit.

the differences, differences that go far beyond the divergence in opening consonant, and involve both formal features and conceptual context. He notes the following: 1. Of the 25 occurrences of *'ôy* in the
MT (Eccles 10 16 cj. and Ps 120 5, איה included), 22 are followed by ל,
of which 19 add a pronominal suffix or its substitute (נפשם, Is 3 9),
usually in the first or second, rarely (Is 3 9 Ez 7 13 9 12) in the third
person. Usually a motivating clause follows, 13 times introduced by
כי. 2. While *hôy* is limited to the prophetic books, *'ôy* shows a much
wider distribution. 3. In contrast to *hôy*, *'ôy* is always referred to
specific persons who, therefore, need not be characterized further.
It gains its real meaning from the clause motivating it. Wanke characterizes it as an *Angst- und Klageruf*, with fluid transition[85]. *Hôy*, by
contrast, arose from more conscious reflection, which leads Wanke to
the happy formulation:

> Das wohl ursprünglich der Totenklage zugehörige הוי soll deutlich machen'
> daß einem bestimmten menschlichen Verhalten der Keim des Todes bereits innewohnt.[86]

This delineates well the conscious and careful differentiation
between the two words in the MT, though a few passages do not
conform, some of which Wanke also notes. In the light of the results
of the earlier part of this chapter we are surprised at this differentiation; we would have expected to meet the "*hôy*-function" and the
"'*ôy*-function" in the same particle(s). The translators of LXX treat
the two words indiscriminately[87]. Certain of the atypical passages
also appear to indicate some crossing of lines. *'Ôy* without ל occurs
in Num 24 23 and Ez 24 6. 9. The latter two instances exhibit not only
the particle-plus-noun structure frequent in *hôy* (cf. an almost identical הוי עיר דמים, Nah 3 1), but also stand in a context that will be
shown below[88] to be characteristic for *hôy*.

    Hôy, for its part, appears in atypical constructions in Jer 30 7[89]
48 1 50 27 Ez 13 3 13 18. In each case but the first a preposition is

---

[85] We have used *Klageruf* in the sense of "cry of mourning within the funerary context" and have, to avoid confusion, employed *Schreckruf*, with the intention of
embracing with it the two aspects pointed out by Wanke. It is an attempt at clarifying
the terminology; as to the matter itself, we are in full agreement with Wanke.

[86] Wanke 218.

[87] Of interest is the woe-series in Hab 2, where the LXX uses οὐαί and ὤ in alternating
order. This shows that the two are considered to be synonyms and that variation has
been the selecting principle. Both of these Greek words are also used to render *'ôy*.
In addition, each renders a series of less common exclamations, such as הי, אי, אהה,
etc.

[88] See below, 77f.

[89] This הוי is generally considered a transposition of היו, with LXX. A balanced bi-
colon could result. On the other hand, the niphal of הפך is characteristically followed
by a preposition, generally ל, as in the present MT reading of Jer 30 6f. To make the

involved: אל, על, and ל respectively. In the first three a כי introduces
a motivating statement, as is normal for 'ôy. It is interesting to note
that two of these atypical hôy-words stand in Ezekiel, making a concentration of four out of eight atypical occurrences of 'ôy/hôy in that
book. The formula in Jer 48 1 stands in a tradition of Moab-oracles,
a tradition which includes the old war song of Num 21 27-30[90], where
the introductory word of verse 29 is 'ôy, however! Jer 48 45-46 takes
up this song, partly verbatim, including the 'ôy-formula, in a context
that seems to indicate a return to the beginning of the chapter where
hôy is employed instead.

We believe the following hypothesis to account plausibly for the
relationships of 'ôy and hôy in the light of the data presented: At an
early date in Israel's history each of the two words, if hôy existed at
all, had both the "'ôy-function" and the "hôy-function". This situation is preserved in Num 21 29 and 24 23. At some later time, probably in some connection with the adoption of the mourning-cry by
the prophets, the word(s) entered a specialized function in prophecy,
as a consequence of which the "prophetic woes" and the general usage
were separated out according to the criteria analyzed by Wanke.
Unless both words existed side by side earlier already[91], it is quite
thinkable that the slight phonetic and/or orthographical differentiation was introduced in this connection. The leveling through was
done systematically, except in the Book of Ezekiel. At least Jer 48 1,
but perhaps also 30 7 50 27 and Ez 13 3. 18 represent "overcorrection"
due to the prophetic context. The use of prepositions after hôy could
then be seen as an incomplete leveling through, rather than as indi-
cating the result of a gradual development of hôy from lamentation
to curse, as suggested by Gerstenberger[92], and Clifford[93], though the
theory of development in the use of hôy need not be implicated as
such. By LXX times the specialized prophetic hôy was not clearly
discerned any longer, and the two words flowed together again into

---

ל dependent on היו is ill-advised. Perhaps the isolated הוי was introduced precisely
to fill the bi-colon metrically. If it were original, as we are inclined to believe, the
context of self-lamentation as well as the subsequent כי-clause would suggest an
original אוי. One is even tempted to wonder whether a לי has not fallen out by homoioteloiton.

[90] For a recent study of this song, see P. D. Miller, Holy War and Cosmic War in Early
Israel (Harvard Dissertation, 1963, unpublished).

[91] Here one might think of the existence, side by side, of Akkadian ū'a and aja, a situation for which 'ôy and hôy seem to lack sufficient contrast, although there are instances of pairs of interjections governed more by assonance than by contrast; cf.
English ah-ha, or German taunting o-ho!

[92] Gerstenberger, The Woe-Oracles, 255, including note 22.

[93] R. J. Clifford, The Use of Hôy in the Prophets, CBQ 28 (1966), 458—464.

the broad common stream from which they had separated out and which is characteristic of such interjections generally[94].

IV. *Hôy* in the Mourning-Vengeance Pattern

The starting point for our investigation of *hôy* was its undisputed rootedness in funerary lament. From that anchor point we have moved out to discover a complex of interjections governed by dynamics that make their interrelations coherent and understandable. It remains a fact, however, that the prophetic woes, though linked to the *hôy* of lamentation much more closely now than usually allowed, contain a strong component of vehement accusation which has led interpreters again and again to seek some association with the curse. It will be our next task to ask whether the realm of lamentation for the dead does not provide dimensions which might allow us to draw these prophetic *hôy*-words also into the circle considered so far and to establish organic relationships between them and the interjections studied.

Where in that realm, we ask, does sorrow, mourning and wailing on the one hand meet with accusation, announcement of evil to come, and curse? They meet where, in the face of violent death, mourning for the dead shades over into cursing of the guilty. This is a widespread practice. Hedwig Jahnow says:

> If a case of murder is involved, the voice of public justice is often raised over the bier of the dead in the form of the funerary lament. Here mourning becomes accusation, and often the name of the murderer is first heard from the lips of the mourning woman.[95]

This shading over from sorrowful funerary lament on the one hand to invective against, yes, curse of, the guilty on the other embraces the whole range of content and mood found in the hôy-passages, a range which offers a genuine *Sitz im Leben* as the home of *hôy*, and which establishes an organic relationship between its apparently so diverse usages.

Striking corroboration for this hypothesis comes from the Ugaritic Legend of Aqhat. Dnil has received word that Aqht is dead, and he

---

[94] G. Fohrer considers the possibility of an original dialectal differentiation between *'ôy* and *hôy* (Prophetie and Magie, ZAW 78, 1966, 38). This may well have been the case, but in the MT the distinction is much more deliberate, as Wanke's analysis shows.

[95] Jahnow 88; my translation. For elaboration of this theme see ibid. 88f. and Heinisch, Totenklage, 25f. The latter contains a beautiful more recent example, including the motif of reversal of fate and the image of the cup (Hab 2 15f.): "Seine Frauen lassen wir trinken, was wir getrunken haben."

has found his remains in the inwards of Sml, Mother of the Eagles.
He weeps and buries Aqht, utters a curse against the eagles, and then
proceeds to curse the place where Aqht lived (*qrt. ablm*) and two other
places(?):

> . . . the king doth *curse*:
> "Woe to thee, O Qiru-mayim,
> O[n] which rests the blood-guilt of Aqhat the Youth!
> . . . the dwellers of the house of El;
> Now, *tomorrow*, and for evermore,
> From now unto all generations!"
> *Again he waves* the staff of his hand,
> And comes to Marurat-taghullal-banir.
> He lifts up his voice and cries:
> "Woe to thee, Marurat-taghullal-banir,
> On which rests the blood-guilt of Aqhat the Youth!
> Thy root grow not in the earth;
> In uprooter's hand droop thy head —
> Now, *tomorrow*, and for evermore,
> From now unto all generations!"
> *Again he waves* the staff of his hand,
> And comes to the city of Abelim,
> Abelim the city of Prince Yarikh.
> He lifts up his voice and cries:
> "Woe to thee, city of Abelim,
> On which rests the blood-guilt of Aqhat the Youth!
> May Baal make thee blind
> From now for evermore,
> From now unto all generations!"[96]

Thereupon Dnil goes to his palace, where elaborate mourning rites
begin.

The word translated as "Woe" is *y*. In each case it is found in
the combination *ylk(m)*. It may well occur in one other lament passage, but as it stands immediately before a break the restoration is
uncertain:

> Anath, [seeing] his vigor extinguished —
> [The vigor of] Aqhat — doth weep.
> "*Woe*! [Would] I could heal [thy corse]!
> . . ."[97]

---

[96] ANET 154f. Transliteration in Andrée Herdner, Corpus des Tablettes en Cunéiformes Alphabétiques, I 1963, Text 19, lines 152—162, p. 90. Transcription and plate
ibid., II 1963, Fig. 61; Pl. XXIX—XXX.

[97] From The Legend of Aqhat, ANET 153. The photograph copy and transcription of
Herdner (Corpus des Tablettes en Cunéiformes Alphabétiques, 1963, Text No. 18)
do not offer much help (Vol. I, No. 18; and Vol. II, Plate XXVIII). She transcribes
y(l/d/ u) [. . .] (Vo.. II, 86).

If the same word were employed, it would offer evidence for the usage of the same short exclamation in mourning where no curse is involved, as in curses against the murderer.

Y also occurs as a vocative particle "O" at least 18 times in combinations such as *yšpš* (O Sun), *ybn* (O Son), *yilm* (O gods), etc. Should the restoration of the above fragment be incorrect, there would still be evidence, then, that a short exclamatory word is used to express a curse of vengeance in a context of mourning. A semantic and/or linguistic connection between Ugaritic *y* and *hôy* suggests itself immediately in the Aramaic וְי "O! oh! woe!" used in the Targum for the *hôy* of Hab 2, for example[98].

Several further features are noteworthy: Dnil's curses are directed against places as is *hôy* in several instances[99]. They occur in a series, as is characteristic for *hôy*. They are spoken in direct address, just as the *hôy*-words must often be interpreted[100]. The combination *ylk* is analogous to the usage found with *'ôy*[101].

This transition from mourning to revenge can be substantiated from other cultures, as it is a widespread feature of the funerary rites discussed in connection with the simple *Klageruf* already. The lamentation of Marduk over Babylon in the Era Epic, quoted at some length[102], offers further evidence. Immediately preceding Marduk's lamentation stands a description of Era's devastation of the city, concluding:

> Ihr [der Bewohner von Babylon] Blut ließest
> du [Era] wie Regenwasser den Marktplatz
> überströmen.

---

[98] Aramaic also has וָיָה and other vocalizations in various Targum editions, as well as וַי, וֵי, וָיָא, and הוֹי, אוֹי, תָּי, הָה. While this variety, just as the Hebrew list, is almost too great to permit specific analysis, we note in both languages the existence of forms where an *a* follows the otherwise final *y*. F. Schulthess (Zurufe an Tiere im Arabischen, 1912, 42f.) observes, on the basis of modern analogies, that exclamatory vowel sounds, when closing softly, tend to develop a final *y* which in all probability receives the accent. If he is correct, this would explain a vowel formation subsequent to it, and the loss or instability of the first syllable. (Of course, one could visualize a similar relationship in reverse order.) The vowel following the *y* could be determined by dissimilation from the last vowel of the first syllable, or if no such syllable existed, by colouring from the opening consonant. Schulthess also points to the practice of labialization of the vowel in a simple consonant-vowel sequence (35f.).

[99] Is 18 1 Nah 3 1 Zeph 3 1. The multiplicity of places in Dnil's curses basically represent a unity: the location of the guilt or the guilty. Cf. David's curse on the "mountains of Gilboa", II Sam 1 21, as well as Lam 4 21.

[100] Cf. above, 22f.

[101] 21 out of 24 instances of אוֹי are constructed with the preposition לְ followed by a personal pronoun, which refers to the first person singular or plural in 10 instances.

[102] See above, 6f.

> Ihre 'Adern' öffnetest du und ließest (das Blut)
> den Fluß hinabfliessen.

Then Marduk's entry follows:

> Der Herr, der Fürst Marduk, sah es und
> sagte: ,,Wehe!" Es ging ihm zu Herzen.
> Ein unlösbarer Fluch lag auf seinen Lippen.
> Er tat einen Schwur: des Flusses Wasser
> trinkt er nicht.
> Ihr Blut sieht er: nicht tritt er ein in
> Esagil.[103]

Then he breaks out into his sevenfold woe. The "Wehe!" just quoted is the u_8-a familiar to us already. It is occasioned by the perdition of his city and its subjects, and it reverts to funerary lamentation in the sevenfold lamentation that follows. These woes phase into a curse, however, a curse that can only be directed against the "murderer"[104], unless, indeed, it is not directed at all, but comes as a reflex to the situation, which would constitute even stronger evidence for the woe-curse pattern[105]. That we are not dealing with a one-time individual-istic composition, but with a pattern, is further supported by the fact that Enlil, in an almost identical passage, also laments his city and then pronounces a curse[106]. The dynamic field of the woe is nicely rounded out by its use in an "'ôy-function" in an expression of sorrow and compassion:

> Es hörte Išum diese seine (Rede)[107];
> Da ergriff ihn Mitleid und er sagte
> (zu sich selber):
> 'Wehe den Menschen, denen Era grollt
> und . . .
> Denen Nergal wie am Tage der Schlacht
> Das Todeslos (verhängt ?).[108, 109]

---

[103] Gössmann 28, lines 35—39. Akkadian 29 (My italics, W. J.).

[104] Thus Gössmann 78.

[105] This possibility was suggested to me by Prof. W. L. Moran.

[106] Gössmann 22, lines 4—9. Akkadian 23.

[107] Era's threat, perhaps against Babylon already, after the destruction of Nippur.

[108] Ibid. lines 29—31. (My italics, W. J.). "Wehe" is u_8-a again.

[109] It is tempting to adduce as further evidence a passage from the Gilgamesh Epic, in von Soden's translation:

> Auf stieg Ischtar auf Uruk-Garts Mauer.
> Sie sprang auf . . ., stieß ein Wehgeschrei aus:
> "Weh über Gilgamesch, der mich beschmäht hat!
> Den Himmelsstier erschlug er!"

(A. Schott, Das Gilgamesch-Epos, durchgesehen und ergänzt von W. von Soden, 1958, 58, Tablet VI, lines 157—159). The Akkadian of the woe-line reads: al-lu-u ^{ilu}Gilgamiš ša u-tab-bil-an-ni GUD.AN.NA id-duk (R. C. Thompson, The Epic of

The lamentation-curse pattern is beautifully illustrated by the Curse over Akkade, where lengthy lamentation finally turns into a long curse beginning:

> Enlil, die Stadt, die deine Stadt zerstört hat,
> möge wie deine Stadt werden,
> die (Stadt), die dein giguna zu einem nichts
> gemacht hat, möge wie Nippur werden.[110]

While a series of *Klagerufe*, "Ach meine Stadt!", etc. precedes this by a few lines[111], these woes are not tied into a close literary unit with the curse, and the passage can therefore be used to illustrate the general pattern only.

That pattern is attested very widely, particularly in cultures where blood vengeance was practiced. The classical Greek tragedies offer many examples. Lasaulx considers the Erinnyes the personified curses of vengeance, as they are identified with the Ἀραί in the classical tragedies[112]. A passage from Aeschylus' Eumenides is instructive in showing how the cries of woe may have accompanied the curse of revenge and underscored it.

> Shame [ἰώ]![113] Ye younger gods, ye have ridden down the ancient laws and have wrested them from my grasp. And I, bereft of honour, unhappy that I am, in my grievous wrath, in requital for my griefs discharge from my heart upon this land (and woe unto it!) [φεῦ ἰὸν ἰὸν . . .] venom, yea venom, in drops its soil can not endure. And from it a canker, blasting leaf, blasting child (ah! [ἰώ] just return!), speeding over the land shall cast upon the ground infection ruinous to human kind. I groan aloud. What shall I do? I am mocked by the people. Intolerable are the wrongs I have suffered. Ah [ἰώ], cruel indeed the wrongs of the woeful daughters of Night, bereft of honour and distress![114]

This curse is repeated again after a consoling speech of Athena and followed by a further curse of vengeance involving various "woes"[115].

Gilgamish, 1930, 41). Our case would rest on the correctness of von Soden's understanding of *allû* as "woe" (cf. also his Grundriß der akkadischen Grammatik, 179, paragraph 124c, where he adds a question mark, and his Akkadisches Handwörterbuch, in loco). As this would be the only occurrence of *allû* as "woe", it may be safer to read a demonstrative adjective: "that Gilgāmeš" (with The Assyrian Dictionary, Volume A, 358, under "allû" (c)).

[110] Falkenstein, Fluch über Akkade, 72, lines 215ff. Note the "reversal of imagery;" see below, 35ff.

[111] See above, 12.

[112] E. v. Lasaulx, Der Fluch bei den Griechen und Römern, Studien des classischen Altertums, 164ff.

[113] Literally, "woe/alas".

[114] Eumenides, lines 778—792, in Aeschylus, II 1926 (with an English translation by H. Weir), in the Loeb Classical Series.

[115] Ibid. lines 808—822. 837—847.

It is interesting that the lamenting ἰώ is used here in self-lamentation, i. e. in an "'ὄy-function," which then becomes indictment and vengeance. The opening ἰώ in this repeated curse stands in a formally fixed position already, while the other two show the more spontaneous accompaniment of the curse by woe-cries.

Arabic provides many examples. Women sing this over the body of a slain young man:

> Legt über den Getöteten das Zelt,
> das Zelt des Getöteten sieht rot aus!
> O (jâ) wäre doch sein Mörder ein Gemordeter,
> sein Blut fließe über des andern Blut![116]

The country of blood vengeance *par excellence* has been Corsica. Gregorovius[117] has described its mourning customs vividly, customs that correspond so closely to the ancient Near Eastern ones that it is not irrelevant to adduce from them evidence for our purpose. Gregorovius describes the transition from lamentation to vengeance:

> Das Wesen dieser Klageweiber hat etwas dämonisches, und muß fürchterlich erscheinen, wenn ihr Tanz und ihre Klage einem Gemordeten gilt. Dann werden sie wahrhaft zu den Furien, den schlangenhaarigen Rächerinnen des Mordes, wie sie Aeschylus gemalt hat. So schwingen sie sich um grausenhaft, die Haare los, die Hände ineinander schlagend, heulend, Rache singend, und so gewaltig ist oft die Wirkung ihres Liedes auf den Mörder, der es hört, daß es ihn mit allen Schauern des Entsetzens und der Gewissensangst erfaßt, und er sich selbst verrät.[118]

In the Old Testament the movement from lamentation over the dead to cursing of the guilty appears also. David's lament over Saul and Jonathan contains a curse of Mt. Gilboa (II Sam 1 21), just as Dnil implicates the location in the murder. After the assassination of Abner David concludes his mourning speech: "The Lord requite the evildoer according to his wickedness!" (II Sam 3 39). The mourning of Lam 1 leads to a prayer of vengeance (verses 21f.; cf. 3 58-66 and Ps 137).

We conclude this survey of a pattern by summarizing it in the words of an exquisite artist who — though remote in time and place from the ancient Near East — knew life and could formulate what is eternally human. Johannes von Tepl lost his wife Margaretha, lamented her passing, and then turned against the last enemy, Death:

---

[116] Dalman 328. Note the reversal of imagery. For further vengeance songs over the dead, see 336; Musil 440 (reversal of imagery), 439. 441. 35f.; Kahle 375 (reversal of imagery). T. Canaan makes the interesting observation that in modern Palestine the address with a term of negative connotation is in itself a curse: "ya hmar ibn ehmar, 'O donkey, son of a donkey;'" "ya harami (nassal), 'O robber (pickpocket);' etc. (The Curse in Palestinian Folklore 256f.). The addressed is often represented by a participle (ibid. 259).

[117] Gregorovius, Corsica, II 1854.   [118] Ibid. 31.

> Oh, Oh, Oh, infamous murderer, Death,
> vile maw of iniquities,
> may the hangman be your judge
> and bind you on his block before me
> as you cry for pardon![119]

Having established a pattern of transition from funerary lament to threat of vengeance, a pattern within which the *Klageruf* can acquire curse-like quality, we turn to the *hôy* pericopes of the Old Testament for direct evidence of such a pattern. A noteworthy passage is Is 1 21-26:

> How the faithful city
>> has become a harlot,
>> she that was full of justice!
> Righteousness lodged in her,
>> but now murderers.
> Your silver has become dross,
>> your wine mixed with water.
>
> . . .
>
> Therefore the Lord says,
>> the Lord of hosts,
>> the Mighty One of Israel:
> Ah (*hôy*), I will vent my wrath on my enemies
>> and avenge myself on my foes.
> I will turn my hand against you
>> and will smelt away your dross as with lye
>> and remove all your alloy.[120]
>
> . . .

Verses 21-23 are a funerary lament, even though the image of death is replaced by that of harlotry. No outside murderer has "killed" the faithful city; the officials within are responsible. Against them the

---

[119] Johann von Tepl, Death and the Ploughman, translated and edited by K. W. Maurer, Preface 1947, 16. This famous mediaeval dialogue dates from the year 1400. The German original reads:
> Ach, ach, ach! vnuerschamter morder, herr Tot,
> boser lasterbalg!
> der zuchtiger sei ewr richter
> vnd binde euch sprechende
> 'vergib mir' in sein wigen!

Johannes von Tepl, Der Ackermann aus Böhmen, ed. by M. O. C. Walshe, 1951, 12. A more recent poetic formulation of this pattern is Uhland's Des Sängers Fluch, where murder is followed by a threefold woe, directed at the scene of the crime and culminating in the curse of the murderer himself: "Weh dir, verruchter Mörder! du Fluch des Sängertums!" Even the "reversal of imagery" is implicitly contained in the last epithet: He who has been a curse to the bards is now hit by the curse of a bard.

[120] For further form-critical and exegetical discucsion of this passage, see below, 57 ff.

Lord hurls a *hôy* of vengeance[121]. Read in the light of our hypothesis, Is 33 1[122] can be readily seen also as a curse of vengeance on the murderer of nations.

We might further introduce an *'ôy*-passage here, Ez 24 6-14. While it is prose, the elements pertinent to our discussion stand out clearly:

> Woe (*'ôy*) to the bloody city, to the pot whose rust is in it . . . For the blood she has shed is still in the midst of her; she put it on the bare rock, she did not pour it upon the ground to cover it with dust. To rouse my wrath, to take vengeance, I have set on the bare rock the blood she has shed, that it may not be covered. Therefore thus says the Lord God: Woe (*'ôy*) to the bloody city! . . . Heap on the logs, kindle the fire . . . you shall not be cleansed any more till I have satisfied my fury upon you . . .[123]

Here we have the blood guilt, the vengeance, and the "reversal of imagery"[124].

There is circumstantial evidence beyond that already advanced. It is noteworthy that *hôy* is often spoken to someone who has "killed", literally or figuratively (Is 10 5 33 1 Nah 3 1 Jer 23 1 Hab 2 12, etc.). This "killer" is often one who has escaped, as it were, or in some way deems himself to be safe from the avenger (Amos 6 1 Is 5 18f. 10 14 29 15 Hab 2 9 Jer 48 7). In several instances an avenger is summoned or sent by the Lord, though in other instances God himself is the one who avenges: "Woe to the proud crown of the drunkards of Ephraem . . . Behold, the Lord has one who is mighty and strong . . ." (Is 28 1f.; cf. also Is 17 12 Nah 3 2 Hab 2 7 Jer 50 25f. 51 1).

---

[121] The verb used here is *nāqām*. G. E. Wright cautions: "The term *nāqām* should not be translated as 'vengeance.' As G. E. Mendenhall has pointed out in an unpublished study, it is divine vindication, which may be punishment or salvation depending on the context." (The Lawsuit of God: A Form-Critical Study of Deuteronomy 32, in: Israel's Prophetic Heritage, ed. by B. W. Anderson and W. Harrelson, 1962, 31, n. 19).

If we have, nevertheless, retained the traditional translation "vengeance" here and in some other places, we have done so to heighten the reader's awareness — at the risk of overemphasis — of the relationship between certain *hôy*- contexts and the extension of the use of *hôy* from its funerary setting into expressions of revenge.

It goes without saying that "vengeance/revenge", where God is the subject, acquires a very different ethical and emotional tone than that which we associate with human revenge, "blood vengeance", etc. We can do no better than to cite Nah 1 2-3 as a commentary on that different tone.

[122] Quoted above, 22.

[123] For further form-critical and exegetical discussion, see below, 77f.

[124] "Reversal of imagery" will be discussed below.

V. "Reversal of Imagery"

Both Is 1 21-26 and Ez 24 6-14 show a further feature worthy of our attention, a feature that we will call, somewhat loosely, "reversal of imagery"[125]: Divine verdicts over sinful behaviour are expressed not only in terms of general punishment, but in terms which take up the very terminology or imagery of the indictment. Is 33 1 illustrates this so clearly that we may be excused for quoting it here once more:

> Woe to you, destroyer (שׁוֹדֵד),
>> who yourself have not been destroyed (שָׁדוּד);
> you treacherous one (בּוֹגֵד),
>> with whom none has dealt treacherously (וְלֹא־בָגְדוּ־בָךְ)!
>
> When you have ceased to destroy (שָׁדוֹד ?),
>> you will be destroyed (תּוּשַׁד);
> and when you have made an end of dealing,
>> treacherously (כִּכַלֹּתְךָ לִבְגֹּד),
> you will be dealt with treacherously (יִבְגְּדוּ בָךְ).

Other *hôy*-pericopes exhibiting this feature are[126]:

> Woe to those who join house to house . . .
> . . . many houses shall be desolate
>> (Is 5 8 . . . 9)
>
> Woe . . . run after strong drink
> . . . dying of hunger . . . parched with thirst.
>> (Is 5 11 . . . 13)
>
> Woe, Assyria, the rod of my anger, the
>> staff of my fury . . .
>
> Shall the ax vaunt itself . . . as if a rod
>> should wield him who lifts it, or as
>> if a staff . . .
>> (Is 10 5 . . . 15)
> Woe to the proud crown of the drunkards of
>> Ephraim, and to the fading flower . . .

---

[125] H. W. Wolff, in a study different in its main concerns but relevant to our subject, has established a typology of these "innerstilistische Beziehungen des sittlichen Urteils" (Die Begründung der prophetischen Heils- und Urteilssprüche, ZAW NF 11, 1934, 16f.). Cf. also J. Fichtner, Die ,,Umkehrung" in der prophetischen Botschaft, ThLZ 78 (1953), 459—466.

[126] Our selection below admittedly highlights the phenomenon in question, perhaps to an unfair degree. In places (especially Is 10 5 . . . 15) we may be dealing with composite literary units. Even though a precise and uniform structural relationship of the "reversal of imagery" to the woe is not always as evident as in Is 33 1, however, the accumulation of instances in *hôy*-contexts seems to warrant some attention. Our exegetical survey (chapter 2) will supply the detailed substantiation for this claim.

> The proud crown ... trodden under foot;
>   and the fading flower ... like a
>   first-ripe fig ...
>   (Is 28 1 ... 3f.)

> Woe, Ariel, Ariel, the city where David encamped ...
> And I will encamp against you ...
>   (Is 29 1 ... 3)

> Woe to him who heaps up what is not his own ...
> Because you have plundered many nations,
>   all the remnant of the peoples shall plunder you ...
>   (Hab 26 ... 8)

> Woe to him who makes his neighbours drink ...
> Drink, yourself, and stagger!
>   (Hab 2 15f.)

Interpreters have treated this phenomenon as a part of the more general tendency of the prophets to present God's punishment as being specific and setting in at the point of transgression[127]. "Reversal of imagery" is indeed widespread, yet not universal in prophecy, as Wolff acknowledges[128]. Further, both Wolff and Fichtner draw heavily on *hôy*-pericopes to illustrate this phenomenon[129]. We are, therefore, justified in asking concerning the more precise literary-cultural background of such speech.

Lohfink has addressed himself to this problem in connection with a study of Hos 4 4-6[130], in particular, verse 6:

> My people are destroyed for lack of knowledge;
> because you have rejected (מָאַסְתָּ) knowledge,
> I reject (אֶמְאָסְאךָ) you from being a priest to me.
> And since you have forgotten (תִּשְׁכַּח) the law
>   of your God,
> I also will forget (אֶשְׁכַּח) your children.

---

[127] Cf. G. von Rad, Theologie des Alten Testaments, II 1965, 83: "Was er [der Empfänger des Drohworts] aber verstehen soll, ist dies, daß das auf ihn zukommende Geschehen als Strafe sehr genau seiner Versündigung entspricht, daß also in der Geschichte von Jahwe her eine Nemesis waltet, oder besser alttestamentlich ausgedrückt: daß das von dem Menschen in Bewegung gebrachte Böse von Jahwe selbst in einer strengen Entsprechung auf sein Haupt zurückgelenkt wird." Fichtner, in Die „Umkehrung", discusses this phenomenon as characteristic for Isaiah. Also Wolff, Die Begründung, passim, and Westermann 114f.

[128] This is evident to any reader of the prophetic books. Wolff also says, "Es ist nicht notwendig, daß die Strafe da einsetzt, wo die Sünde liegt ...," (Die Begründungen 15).

[129] See the articles cited above, n. 125.

[130] N. Lohfink, Zu Text und Form von Os 4 4-6, Bibl 42 (1961), 303—332.

He rejects Wolff's characterization of it as *Talionstil*[131] by limiting that term to the equation "noun for noun"[132], although he is ready to recognize a "wurzelhaften Zusammenhang von Stil und Stimmung" between the *Talionstil* and the style of the Hosea-pericope and to accomodate both within a *"Talionsdenken"*:

> Die Talionsformeln und Os 4 5f. sind nur zwei Punkte innerhalb eines weiten Formen- und Aussagefeldes, in denen sich das „Talionsdenken" durch Wortwiederholungen ausdrückt.[133]

At the same time, he claims a difference:

> Vor allem in [Hos] 4 5b — 6a, aber auch in den anderen Zeilen bewirkt erst die Doppelung der Tätigkeitsworte, daß Vorder- und Nachsatz den Eindruck machen, sie entsprächen einander. Die Identität des Tätigkeitsworts wirkt aufdeckend. Die im Wesen der Einzelhandlung noch nicht sichtbare göttliche Straffolge wird sprachlich ans Licht gezaubert und damit schlagend bewiesen. Demgegenüber befassen sich die wirklichen Talionsformeln und auch Gn 9 6a mit einer von vornherein im Wesen der Tat angelegten und daher auch aus ihr sprachlich ableitbaren Nemesis.[134]

One cannot doubt that this differentiation describes correctly the extremes of a continuum. That there is a middle ground where the two meet proceeds from Lohfink's own example, of a *Talionsformel* developed into a *vollen Rechtssatz*, Gen 9 6a, of the *Talionstil*[135]:

> He who sheds man's blood
> by man shall his blood be shed!

Formally, we have here a doubling of the verb, as well as the nouns. As to content, it is questionable whether the subsequent retaliation is "von vornherein im Wesen der Tat angelegt", any more than in Hos 4 6, if one assumes the latter to stand as firmly within the legal structure of the covenant as the former within the legal structure of interpersonal relationships.

Another form, which is grouped into the *Talionsdenken* by Lohfink[136], is scarcely represented in the Old Testament[137], but is extant in Near Eastern literature; it is the curse of the type found in the *Klmw*-Inscription:

---

[131] H. W. Wolff, Dodekapropheton I. Hosea, 1961, 91. Cf. also O. Eißfeldt, The Old Testament, translated by P. R. Ackroyd, 1965, 68.

[132] Cf. Ex 21 23 Lev 24 18-20 Deut 19 21; but also in prophetic contexts: I Kings 20 42. In Gen 96a it has developed into a "vollen Rechtssatz". A. Alt's conclusions lend support to this emphasis on the noun (Zur Talionsformel, ZAW 52, 1934, 303—305).

[133] Lohfink 313.

[134] Ibid.

[135] Eißfeldt, The Old Testament, loc. cit.

[136] Lohfink 314f.

[137] Although Ps 137 5 approaches it, according to Lohfink (315).

> Wer diese Inschrift zerschlägt —
>> sein Haupt zerschlage Ba'l-Samad von Gabar,
>> sein Haupt zerschlage Ba'l-Hamman von
>> Bmh und Rakabel, der Ba'l des Hauses![138]

A further type, according to Lohfink, is connected with indictment for breach of the laws of Holy War: Josh 7 25 I Sam 15 33. With this we move into the covenant context. The breaking in of the covenant curses can be described in Deuteronomistic language as follows:

> They despised (וַיִּמְאֲסוּ) his statutes,
>> and his covenant that he made with
>> their fathers,
>> and the warnings which he gave them . . .
> And the Lord rejected (וַיִּמְאַס) all the
>> descendants of Israel . . .
>> (II Kings 17 15.20)

The purpose of our review of Lohfink's findings is to show that the phenomenon which we have called with the broad name "reversal of imagery" occurs in a network of related settings well designated by Lohfink as *Talionsdenken:* 1. Blood vengeance. 2. Word magic operative to reveal an inner connection and establish the consequences through a linguistic necessity (Hos 4 6 etc.). 3. Curses. 4. The reversal of *ḥerem* onto the head of him who breaks the law of Holy War. 5. The reversal of covenant curses against the covenant breaker. It is in this circle of *Talionsdenken,* we hold, that the "reversal of imagery" of the *hôy*-pericopes is at home. It is not the monopoly of the lamentation-vengeance sequence[139], of course, nor is it an absolutely essential feature of that sequence, but the fact that it does occur repeatedly in the *hôy*-pericopes strengthens our association, argued on other grounds already, of these pericopes with the realm of retaliatory retribution[140].

---

[138] Lohfink 314. A photostatic reproduction of the original, as well as a transliteration and translation, the latter with introduction and commentary, are accessible in H. Donner and W. Röllig, Kanaanäische und aramäische Inschriften, 1962—1964, vol. III plate XXVII, vol. I 4f., and vol. II 30ff., respectively. The verb forms which carry the interplay of deed and vengeance are *jšḥt-jšḥt-wjšḥt.*

[139] It is interesting to note that Wolff (Dodekapropheten 91. 96) considers Hos 4 6a an "anklagende Klage", thus offering a further, though small, item of support for the association of lamentation, accusation, and the reversal of imagery.

[140] Extra-Biblical evidence for the place of this "reversal of imagery" in the lamentation-retaliation pattern exists in abundance. E. Littmann gives this example:
> Seine [des Mörders] Frauen lassen wir trinken,
> was wir getrunken haben.
> Ali werde heute zum Mörder,
> er, der Gemordete.

We conclude, then that the lamentation-vengeance pattern, a pattern widely attested in various cultures, forms a context within which the woe-cry can undergo a metamorphosis from grief and mourning to accusation, threat, and even curse. Moreover, this metamorphosis is discernible within the Old Testament itself, so that we are able to trace an unbroken continuum in the function of the woe-cry, a continuum which, in arc-like manner, spans those *hôy*-words clearly expressive of funerary lamentation and those which are hurled against a slayer, literal or metaphorical, in a spirit of bitterness and revenge.

Abbessinische Klagelieder 15. Cf. also Dalman 328; Musil 440; Kahle 375. The image of the cup in this connection occurs also in the woe-passage Hab 2 15—16 (cf. Jer 25 17 ff.).

Chapter 2: Exegetical Study of *Hôy*-Pericopes

I. The Approach

It has been the aim of the previous chapter to search for an understanding of *hôy* which would make it possible to place its various and diverse extant usages into a fabric within which they would become intelligible both in their interrelatedness and in their diversification. An investigation of the dynamics of the mourning cry within the context of funerary lament has laid open a range of emotional tone and linguistic-social function extending from vocative address to sorrow and grief and, ultimately, to an indicting cry of revenge sent out after a murderer. This range, widely embracing as it is, never forces us to abandon the primary *Sitz im Leben*, death, funeral and mourning.

It is clear, however, that this primary *Sitz im Leben* has been preserved in only a small number of *hôy*-occurrences in the Old Testament[1]. In the majority of *hôy*-pericopes this word has been adopted into a secondary context. It is the purpose of this and the following chapter to characterize that context and to account, if possible, for that adoption. What place, in other words, did the prophets accord *hôy* in their proclamation? And what was it that induced them to draft *hôy* into it? A form-critical and exegetical survey of *hôy*-pericopes should address itself to the first question and should lay the foundation for considering the second.

There is general consensus concerning the core of the *hôy*-formula, i. e. the fact that it consists of the introductory *hôy* plus an addressee often, but not always, designated in a participial clause paralleled by a second participial clause. Beyond that, however, no objective criterion for delimiting the formula over against its present prophetic context seems discoverable[2]. And yet it is the handling of this delimi-

---

[1] See above, 4.

[2] Contrast with Westermann 139, for example. Westermann calls the initial *hôy*, followed by a participial clause, paralleled by a second participial clause, "eine auffallend feste Form". This is certainly an overstatement tenable only if a number (Westermann: 16) of *hôy*-words have been excluded because of their funerary or vocative character (cf. above, 19f.). Even then the participle is not an altogether firm component of the formula; of the total number of *hôy*'s only 2/5 are followed by a participle! One could argue that the firm "formula" consists of the word *hôy* only, and there are, in fact, several instances where it stands in formal isolation or inde-

tation which predetermines important conclusions concerning the nature and background of the formula. It is the fact, for example, that Gerstenberger excludes from the formula proper any elements that represent direct address which leads him to see in the *hôy*-formula an impersonal wisdom injunction[3]. To break this impasse it is necessary to rephrase the problem. *Instead of asking what ready-coined formula the prophet adopted and where he began to add to it, we ask: Are there signs that the prophet was conscious of the origin of hôy in funerary lament and that he employed it in a manner consonant with or governed by that background?* In pursuit of this question we turn to specific texts, proceeding in a chronological order, as much as possible.

II. Amos 5 18-20 6 1-7

The earliest occurrences of *hôy* are two instances in Amos (5 18 6 1)[4]. The pericope 5 18-20 follows immediately upon the funerary lament of verses 16-17, containing the repeated mourning cry *hô-hô*, generally considered to be a variant of *hôy*. An association between the *hôy* of verse 18 and the *hô-hô* of verse 16 seems likely, but the question arises whether the relationship between the two pericopes cannot be extended beyond the assonance of *hô-hô* and *hôy*, and their present proximity within the somewhat distended yet nevertheless

---

pendence (Is 1 24 17 12 Jer 30 7 Zech 2 10). We hope to clarify the situation in the present chapter.

[3] Gerstenberger, The Woe-Oracles, 249—251. He limits his investigation to certain woe-oracles only, eliminating in this process, first, all those *hôy*-words which are clearly associated with mourning; secondly, the passages where *hôy* introduces "a threat, a pronouncement which not only forecasts a catastrophe but consciously endorses and promotes it;" and thirdly, the passages where *hôy* "is connected with expressions of revenge . . . or of great excitement." This eliminates approximately thirty occurrences of *hôy* from his study.

[4] A *hôy* opening Am 5 7 is a widely accepted conjecture; cf. BHmg. Its loss could easily be explained as haplography. The otherwise grammatically awkward opening of this verse would be removed so as to create a woe of verses 7.10-12. In the light of the *hôy*-pattern of subsequent prophecy such an oracle would seem appropriate in form and content and would lead to a chain of three *hôy*-words (5 7 5 18 6 1). As it lacks any textual support, however, and is built completely on the possibility suggested by 5 18 and 6 1, we can hardly admit it as evidence for the awareness of Amos concerning the background of *hôy*. Against such a conjecture T. H. Robinson argues that 5 7 is a fragment and cannot be related to verse 10, due to difference in content (T. H. Robinson and F. Horst, Die Zwölf Kleinen Propheten, 1964[3], 89f.). For further discussion and literature see K. W. Neubauer, Erwägungen zu Amos 4 4-15, ZAW 78 (1966), 292—316, especially 293 n. 4 and 312—315.

coherent prophetic speech of chapter 5[5]. We believe that it is possible.

The wailing of verses 16-17 is motivated by the prospect that "I [Yahweh] will pass through the midst of you" (אעבר בקרבך). The otherwise very common verb עבר appears six times in the Book of Amos. Three of these merely express movement (5 5 6 2) and the passage of time (8 5), but the remaining three refer to a threatening visitation by the Lord (5 17 7 8 8 2). In the passage under discussion (5 16-17) this visitation will result in wailing and mourning. The other two passages exhibit עבר, identically in the formula לא אוסיף עוד עבור לו. The context, in each case, is a vision through which the Lord announces the finality of his verdict over Israel. These visions again, stand in contrast to the two earlier visions of chapter 7, where the verdict was averted (לא תהיה; 7 3, 6). The consequence of the Lord's passing by no longer, will be desolation of the high places and sanctuaries (7 9 8 3), and the rising of Yahweh himself "against the house of Jeroboam with the sword" (7 9). This "passing by no longer" can mean nothing else than Yahweh's Holy War against his own people[6]. It is possible, further, to interpret the reference to fire as the agent

---

[5] Neubauer (ibid.) has argued on the basis of the expression "the Lord of hosts will be with you, as you have said" (verse 14) that verses 4-15, with the exception of 8-9 and 13, form a unit with an anti-cultic thrust. He understands the cited phrase as a scornful quotation of a formula of weal current in the cultus. If this is so, verses 16-17 would fittingly continue the theme by announcing that weal would turn into woe, feasting into mourning, a reversal proleptically indicated already in the *qînāh* which opens the oration (verses 2-3). Weiser's rearrangement of the content of chapters 5—6 seems both unnecessary and arbitrary (Das Buch der zwölf Kleinen Propheten, I 1967[5], 163—180).

[6] The origin of the concept of Day of the Lord in Israel's Holy War tradition has been argued vigorously by G. von Rad (The Origin of the Concept of the Day of Yahweh, JSS 4, 1959, 97—108), against Mowinckel (Jahves dag, Norsk teologisk Tidskrift 59, 1958, 1—56). The cosmic dimension of the progression from Holy War to the Day of Yahweh has been demonstrated by F. M. Cross, Jr., who traces the motif of Yahweh as Divine Warrior who leads the earthly and the cosmic armies through victorious warfare to the cosmic and cultic manifestation of his glory (The Divine Warrior in Israel's Early Cult, in: Biblical Motifs, ed. by A. Altmann, 1966, 11—30). Cf. also the [unpublished] Harvard dissertation of P. D. Miller, Jr., Holy War and Cosmic War in Early Israel, 1963; and the same, The Divine Council and the Prophetic Call to War, VT 18 (1968), 100—107.

That the warfare of this Day can be directed against Israel herself is the new element in Amos' proclamation (G. von Rad, The Origin of the Concept of the Day of Yahweh, 104f.), an element which becomes a prominent feature of subsequent prophetic preaching (J. A. Soggin, Der prophetische Gedanke über den Heiligen Krieg, als gerichtet gegen Israel, VT 10, 1960, 79—83; G. von Rad, Theologie des Alten Testaments, II 133).

of judgement (7 4)[7] in the context of traditional Holy War terminology[8]. The vision 8 1-3 explicitly designates the visitation as "that day" and associates with it the reversal of songs into wailing and death scenery though the textual difficulties of verse 3 call for caution in its use[9]. This reversal of joy into mourning, light into darkness, forms the description of "that day" 8 9-10 also[10].

---

[7] To draw on this verse in such a way assumes, of course, that the five visions (7 1-3. 4-6. 7-9 8 1-3 9 1-4) form a progression in which the visitation which could be averted through intercession for a while (7 1-3. 4-6) can eventually be averted no longer 7 7-9 8 1-3 9 1-4). The formal difference between the two sets of visions is correctly ascribed by Weiser (Das Buch der zwölf Kleinen Propheten I, 184f.) to this progression in their content.

[8] The prominence of fire in the terminology of Holy War is discussed by P. D. Miller, Jr., Fire in the Mythology of Canaan and Israel, CBQ 27 (1965), 256—261. The phrase לרב באש, though textually well attested, is generally considered to be corrupt. The presence of consuming fire as Yahweh's agent is demanded by text and context, however, whether one emends לְשָׁבִיב אֵשׁ (BHmg), לַהַב אֵשׁ (Robinson), or אֵשׁ לַהֶבֶת (Weiser). The cosmic dimension of Holy War (see above, 42, n. 6), a dimension which embraces every cosmic as well as earthly opponent of the Divine Warrior, allows without difficulty for the object תהום רבה, the Great Deep, and makes an attempt at a naturalistic explanation (Weiser, Das Buch der zwölf Kleinen Propheten I, 183f.) appear somewhat tortuous.

To what extent the locusts of 7 1 (גבי) belong to the formulaic language of the Holy War-Day of Yahweh complex cannot be pursued here. In the war context of Nah 3 15 fire, sword, and locust (ילק, ארבה Nah 3 17) are associated. By the time of Joel fire, locust and the Day of Yahweh had melted into an indissoluble complex. In an Excursus to his commentary on Joel, H. W. Wolff discusses the locust-terminology of the Old Testament, but he omits discussion of the term גבי and ascribes no significance to Am 7 1 beyond one passing reference (Dodekapropheton, Joel, 1963, 30—32).

The understanding of Amos' visions suggested here does not make it necessary to reject altogether the traditional view that concrete observation of locusts, draught, etc., may have sparked Amos' visions. The selection of these particular triggering phenomena from among the countless facets of everyday life would be illumined, however, if our considerations are correct.

[9] Certain formal and textual considerations are necessary in connection with our admission of 7 9 and 8 3 as evidence in the case under discussion. As is generally recognized, a strict formal comparison of the visions 7 7-9 8 1-3 with those of 7 1-3. 4-6 and Jer 1 11-12 reveals a type complete without 7 9 and 8 3. The question arises, then, how to understand the addition of these verses. Weiser (Das Buch der zwölf Kleinen Propheten I, ad locos) sees no connection in form and content between these verses and the preceding visions. He relegates the verses to a later redactor (but compare the inconsistent statement on p. 129!). He sees in 7 9 a later expansion of the vaguely formulated threat of the vision, an expansion closing with a reference to the "house of Jeroboam", meant to be a correction on the basis of history for 7 11, "Jeroboam shall die by the sword". 8 3 is equally secondary, according to Weiser,

We recognize in these passages the mosaic pieces of a pattern: The Lord, as divine warrior, no longer passes by his people[11], but

----

and unrelated to the preceding vision, as is evidenced by the *eschatologische Anknüpfungsformel* "in that day".

This raises the question why the biographical section 7 10-17—displaced from an earlier concluding position in the Amos-collection by the addition of 9 11-15 (ibid. 129—131)—should have been inserted at this point into the midst of the *kleine Visionsschrift* (7 1-9 8 1-3 9 1-4) which Weiser postulates and considers to be the core of the Book of Amos and its only undoubtedly authentic section. Even if the reference to the "house of Jeroboam" were a conscious revision of 7 11 one should expect a similar verse in this place to account for the insertion of 7 10-17, or if verse 9c were an expansion, at least a bi-colon consisting of 9 ab.

Further, the fact that 8 1-2 is also followed by an explication in concrete terms (verse 3), as is Jer 1 13-14 (verses 15ff.), makes it likely that such an explication of the vision is a characteristic accompaniment of the vision, rather than a haphazard redactor's comment. That the visions of 7 1-6 do not have it is the logical result of their content: "It shall not be"; no explication is possible for that which does not happen. Jer 1 11-12, on the other hand, is explicated, together with 1 13-14, by verses 15ff. It is best to see in 7 9 and 8 3 an explication of the terse vision form by Amos himself, as T. H. Robinson seems to understand them (Die Zwölf Kleinen Propheten 99. 101), or at least to recognize in them an expansion which develops consistently from the theology of Amos' proclamation. Rudolph argues for a similar unity of composition for Jer 1 13-16 (Jeremia, 1968[3], ad locum).

H. W. Wolff assumes that 7 9 and 8 3 come from an *alte Amosschule*, consisting of Amos' immediate disciples whose characteristics become clear in the following words concerning the author of 7 10-17: "Der Verfasser muß ein Augen- und Ohrenzeuge gewesen sein. Er trifft Stil und Thematik des Amos ziemlich genau . . ." (Dodekapropheton, Amos, 1967, 131). For the purpose of our investigation such closeness of form and content is sufficient. It is not our task here to evaluate the school-theory as such.

The verse 8 3 is textually corrupt beyond indisputable reconstruction, but certain elements seem clear. We would posit at least a metrically balanced bi-colon as its core (cf. our discussion of 7 9):

7/   יחהילילו שיירות היכל
6/   רב יה־פגר בכל־מקום

Whether שי״רות is vocalized as "songs" (MT), or female singers (BHmg.; Weiser, Robinson), or τὰ φατνώματα (the majority of Greek witnesses), or gates/ στρόφιγγες (BHmg.; Codex W., Aquila) does not affect our argumentation, nor does the specific understanding of היכל and כל־מקום , though a reference to the sanctuaries seems most appropriate. ביום ההוא נאם אדני יהוה appears to be a specifying gloss (cf. 8 9) impossible to fit into any metrically acceptable reconstruction, a gloss, however, which makes explicit the pattern underlying the latter part of the Book of Amos. השליך הס suggests the possibility of an original tri-colon (cf. 7 9), but neither the Greek (ἐπιρρίψω σιωπήν) nor the commentators seem to solve the problem.

[10] The relationship between 8 4-14 and the preceding visions is generally recognized as being a very close one. Robinson (Die Zwölf Kleinen Propheten 70. 102f.) sees in them genuine Amos-oracles, placed here by a redactor. Similarly, Weiser (Das Buch

passes through their midst in his Holy War which turns their feasting (at the shrines) into wailing and mourning in the streets[12]. The *hô-hô* of the mourners of 5 16, predicted to follow the Lord's passing through,

der zwölf Kleinen Propheten I, 130. 196f.) assumes here an early supplementation of the *kleine Visionsschrift* with genuine Amos-words. Wolff (Dodekapropheton, Amos, 132) attributes verses 9f. in particular to the *alte Amosschule* and stresses their closeness to the prophet's speech especially. Weiser is right, of course, when he rejects (196) the tempting assumption that verses 9f. may have belonged together originally with the Day-pericope 5 18ff. The place of each within the Day of the Lord-pattern is not recognized clearly by him ,however, because he lacks a sufficiently comprehensive image of the Holy War-Day of the Lord-sequence.

[11] It may be worth noting that at least one-half of the approximately fifteen passages in which "passing through" is applied to a nation or nations (namely Ex 12 23 15 16 (2×) Num 20 19. 20 Deut 2 18. 28 29 15 Josh 24 17) are associated with Israel's march through the nations in connection with the Exodus and Conquest. Ex 12 23 is a variation on the same theme: The Lord passes through to slay the Egyptians. Especially passages like Ex 12 23 and 15 16 make it tempting to see in עבר, applied to nations, at least a leaning towards technical usage related to the Holy War terminology of the March of Conquest. If that were so, the pronouncements of Amos that the Lord would no longer pass by "my people Israel" (cf. Ex 15 16!), but pass through its midst (Am 7 8 8 2 5 17) could be seen not only as the reversal of Holy War against Israel, but as the re-application of the Conquest-terminology itself. Of interest in this connection is Zeph 2 2, where the Day of the Lord is the subject of עבר. The appearance in Nah 2 1 of the near-identical formula to Am 7 8 and 8 2 indicates that we are dealing with a cliché of war-terminology.

The above suggestions must be made in a very tentative way only, however, in view of the widespread use of עבר, not only in a general sense, but also to express a variety of punishments and scourges (Is 28 15.18.19, Mic 5 7 Ez 5 17, etc.).

[12] H. W. Wolff's incisive and literarily sensitive introductory discussion of the Book of Amos (Dodekapropheton, Amos, 105—138) is replete with insights into various aspects of the pattern which we have characterized, but the implicit assumptions involving the views of the Alt-School concerning the *Landnahme*, the concomitant inability to relate Exodus and Law into a covenant pattern, and the inability of relating Holy War to the Conquest and, consequently, to the reversal of it against Israel, keep him from breaking through to a wide panorama, a *Gesamtbild* with the visitation of the Divine Warrior at the centre. The function of *hôy* in this pattern is further obscured for Wolff by its assignment to the realm of wisdom instruction (summarized again on 112).

In a different context (Amos' geistige Heimat 23) he notes again a relationship of *hôy* to the Day of the Lord: "So ist es auch gar nicht mehr befremdlich, wenn Amos unter den Wehe-Rufen nicht nur Themen wie Rechtsordnung und Rechtsverhalten, Weintrinken, Hochmut, Selbstsicherheit und Luxus, sondern auch das in den Stämmetraditionen vom Krieg Jahwes beheimatete Thema 'Tag Jahwes' abhandelt, und zwar eben in der Sprache und mit dem Anschauungsmaterial der Sippenweisheit." The insight which, for the above-mentioned reasons, cannot quite crystallize, is the recognition of the place of the enumerated themes right within the Holy War-Day of the Lord panorama.

is shown by this pattern to be identical in motivation and content
with the *hôy* of verse 18, called out by the prophet over the secure
people who will be overtaken by the darkness of the Day of the Lord.
In other words, the *hôy* of verse 18 projects a contrast to the expected
Day of light and brightness (verses 18-20), but that contrast consists
of mourning, as the pattern developed from 5 16-17 (or even 5 1-17)
7 7-9 and 8 1-3. 10 requires. The *hôy* of verse 18 is consequently best
understood as a mourning cry.

Am 5 18-20 shows both nearness to and distance from the prophetic *Gerichtswort*[13]. As in the latter, a present state of affairs is
characterized and on its basis a calamity to come is announced.
Formal resemblance to the prophetic *Begründung* and *Ankündigung*
is very tenuous, however. The characterization of the present state
is compressed into the participle המתאוים, "those who wish for", a
participle rendered negative only by the preceding *hôy* and the sub-

---

[13] The terminology used in classifying the subsegments of prophetic speech is not uniform. Gunkel's categories *Scheltwort* (invective/reproach) and *Drohwort* (threat)
have found wide acceptance. They suggest two distinct types of speech, however,
obscuring the underlying unity of the parts in question. To remedy this, Westermann
(Grundformen prophetischer Rede 102—126, with the schematic summary reproduc-
ed here, 122) has suggested the overarching term *Gerichtswort* for the basic form of
prophetic proclamation, with the following sub-classification:

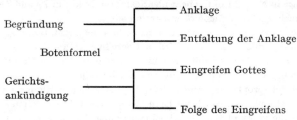

Westermann's translator, H. C. White (Basic Forms of Prophetic Speech, 1967, 171)
has rendered this as follows:
Gerichtswort (judgement-speech):

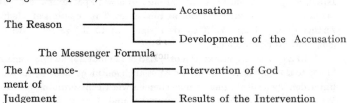

This descriptive rendering does not do full justice to the technical nature of the
terminology. Our own earlier suggestion (The Role of the Prophet, Interpretation 19,
1956, 346) had been "motivation" (for *Begründung*) and "proclamation" (for *Gerichtsankündigung*). In this chapter we have retained Westermann's German terms
Begründung and *Ankündigung*.

sequent announcement. That announcement, again, lacks the usual declarative directness of prophetic verdicts; it is dialogically evoked through the rhetorical questions of verses 18a and 20[14], questions supported in their intent by the comparisons of verse 19[15], introduced to sharpen the contrast between the expected Day and its completely unexpected reality. In spite of this lack of conformity to normal prophetic speech this pericope does not make the impression of casual, formally haphazard structure, as the characteristic initial position of *hôy* as well as the following participle indicate[16]. At this point we merely note these facts and reserve discussion of the *hoy*-form for a later section.

The *hôy*-pericope of Am 6 1-7 begins with *hôy* followed by a participle, balanced by another participle in a parallel colon and followed by a chain of further bi-cola governed by participles or finite verbs[17]. They preserve a rather consistent *parallelismus membrorum*, interrupted only by the imperatives and the rhetorical question of verse 2[18],

[14] Verse 18c is a gloss, of course, prompted by verse 20.

[15] We can readily agree with Wolff when he sees the language of wisdom in these questions and comparisons: "Ist es Zufall, daß Amos die sonst immer in der Welt des großen kriegerischen Erlebens beheimatete Rede vom Tage Jahwes mit der Anschauungswelt des Wanderhirten illustriert?" (Amos' geistige Heimat 11. For a discussion of the questions, see 7 ff.) Here the subservience of individual elements of wisdom speech to a proclamation arising out of an altogether different realm has been realized and acknowledged. When Wolff proceeds, however, to characterize the *hôy*-form as such as belonging to popular wisdom with a didactic aim (12—23), he advocots an understanding radically different from that which emerges in the present study. S. Terrien, on the contrary, does not list the *hôy*-occurrences as evidence of wisdom in Amos (Amos and Wisdom, in: Israel's Prophetic Heritage, ed. by B. W. Anderson and W. Harrelson, 1962, 108—115). Instead, he acknowledges Amos' closeness to covenant theology and the eschatological orientation of his message (114f.), facts which force themselves upon Wolff also (Dodekapropheton, Amos, "Die Botschaft," 121—129), but are hardly acknowledged fully and comprehensively even there (see above, 45, n. 12).

[16] See above, 40, n. 2.

[17] This situation, as well as the text of 6 1-7, has been discussed recently by R. Fey (Amos und Jesaja, 1963, 11—17).

[18] Many interpreters consider this verse to be an expansion. While that cannot be denied categorically, we note both the frequency of rhetorical questions in Amos (cf. Wolff, Amos' geistige Heimat, 7—12) and the common occurrence of such questions in close succession to *hôy*, as in 5 18. 20. Is 10 8f. is particularly interesting due to the similarity of its content to Am 6 2. Other examples are Is 1 5 10 3 29 16 45 9. 11 55 2 Jer 47 3 Ez 13 7. 18 34 2 Hab 2 7. 13. We hasten to add that it is not necessary to follow Wolff (ibid.) in interpreting this phenomenon as a symptom of the wisdom character of *hôy*. Surely such questions are not the peculiar property of wisdom. In most of the passages cited they do not sound didactic at all, but rather menacing, as in a dare flung before an adversary in the heat of controversy or in a foreboding threat of

a question reminiscent of the questions of 5 18-20. As in that oracle,
our passage moves from accusation to announcement, but in spite
of the opening לכן verse 7 can hardly balance formally the lengthy
chain of bi-cola preceding it, so that the pericope makes the impression
of secondary adaption to the *Gerichtswort*, at best. Within that adaption, *hôy* is prophetic, not divine speech.

Its inner dynamic is one of contrast, a contrast between the
overt description of luxurious and satiated feasting on the one hand,
and the unexpected breaking in of calamity upon those deeming themselves secure, a calamity which is foreshadowed already in the opening
hôy itself, in the reference to the fallen neighbouring states (verse 2),
in the "evil day" held at bay (verse 3)[19], and is announced explicitly
in verse 7. The reversal of imagery between ראשית הגוים (verse 1),
וראשית שמנים (verse 6) and בראש גלים (verse 7) gives special focus to
the contrast.

While the technical terminology of mourning is not used—apart
from *hôy* itself—, the whole pericope is governed by that content pattern which we recognized above, a pattern which appears to have its
roots in Amos' image of the Day of the Lord, an image which we cannot
trace beyond Amos, where it presents itself as an announcement of
the unexpected, and which we must, therefore, at least at the present
state of research, consider his own original prophetic message.

There can be little doubt, then, that Amos is fully conscious of the
mourning function of *hôy*, but employs it in anticipation of that
particular mourning and wailing which will be called for by the Day
of the Lord, proclaimed by himself as the day of gloom when the Lord's
Holy War will unexpectedly strike against Israel. In this context

vengeance. It seems quite appropriate to retain verse 2, though the reference to Gath
may be a later addition (Robinson, Die Zwölf Kleinen Propheten, 92. 94; Weiser, Das
Buch der zwölf Kleinen Propheten I, 176).

[19] יום רע is not one of the technical terms for the Day of the Lord (for those terms, see
L. Černý, The Day of Yahweh and Some Relevant Problems, 1948, Appendix I),
but denotes general misfortune, though the plural seems to be preferred (Ps 37 19
49 6 94 13 Prov 15 15 etc.). The nature of the misfortune must be derived from the
context. The context for Am 6 3 points to a situation, however, which leaves no doubt
that the "evil day" cannot be anything else here than that terrible final judgement
which fills the proclamation of Amos and which is called יום יהוה in 5 18-20. To that
passage the content of 6 3 stands in an even closer relation: There the people addressed
wished for the Day (understood as a "good day"); here they wish away the Day
(characterized properly from the prophet's vantage point as an "evil day"). If the
difficult המנדים were to be read with LXX[AQ] (οἱ εὐχόμενοι) as a verb expressing
desire for the day, the parallelism would become even more direct, with the assumption, of course, that the people mistake the "evil day" for a "good day." Robinson
suggests "oder: 'herrufen,' cf. arab. *nadā* (G. R. Driver brieflich)" (Die Zwölf Kleinen
Propheten 92).

hôy acquires a foreboding and threatening quality, while it retains at the same time a considerable formal independence from the prophetic *Gerichtswort*[20].

III. Isaiah: First Series of Woes

The genuine Isaianic woes appear, in the main, in two chains, Is 5 8-24 and Is 28—31, words from the early ministry of Isaiah and from the time of the final Assyrian crisis, respectively. Scattered occurrences are found in 1 4 1 24 10 1 10 5 17 12 and 18 1.

As to form the first chain represents a rather confused picture[21]. Verses 8-10 and 11-13 conform loosely to the prophetic *Gerichtsrede*. We note in each case that the punishment to come constitutes a reversal of the situation, an Isaianic characteristic[22], though not foreign to prophecy generally. In verses 8a and 9b this results in "reversal of

---

[20] Westermann has recognized this tension as characteristic for all "prophetic *hôy* words" when he calls the *hôy*-form the most important and most frequent variant of the prophetic *Gerichtswort* (Grundformen prophetischer Rede 137) and proceeds to point out the variant qualities of the *hôy*-pericopes (137—140). A study of *all* *hôy*-passages (cf. above, 3f. 19) tends to emphasize even more the looseness of their relation to the *Gerichtswort*, as well as their independent inner dynamic.

[21] The longer threat contained in 5 14-16 undoubtedly constitutes an inclusion of material belonging with 2 6-22 (cf. R. B. Y. Scott, Isaiah, in: The Interpreter's Bible, V 1956, 159. 200f.), though verse 14 need not be a part of 15-16. Wildberger (Jesaja, 1956—, ad locum) considers verses 14 and 17 to be the fragmentary remnant of a separate woe-oracle. Even so, all attempts to achieve a sequence of formally balanced woes, uniform in length and meter, fail, and that in spite of a relatively well preserved text and a fairly easily discernible inner structure of each oracle.

The cohesion of this *hôy*-sequence is one of content, as Kaiser points out (Der Prophet Jesaja, Kapitel 1—12, 1963[2], 56; see quotation below, 50). To assume on this basis, with Kaiser (ibid.), even tentatively, a common composition by the prophet seems methodologically improper. Opinion concerning such common origin is completely divided. The same criteria which might support it can also be adduced as the cause for inclusion into a secondary grouping. That the present arrangement (including 10 1-4[a]; see below) was conscious, and perhaps aimed at the number seven, is very likely, in view of the tendency of *hôy* to be repeated in funerary lamentation, as well as the tendency of the extant canonical *hôy*'s to "flock together." We would suggest that Isaiah probably did not speak his woe-oracles in isolation, but rather in "volleys," a fact reflected by the collectors, though the formal differences of the chain under discussion do not allow us to posit an original composition of seven formally uniform woes, a composition subsequently deformed to its present formally heterogeneous state.

[22] J. Fichtner, Die „Umkehrung" in der prophetischen Botschaft. Eine Studie zu dem Verhältnis von Schuld und Gericht in der Verkündigung Jesajas, ThLZ 78 (1953), 459—466.

imagery" (בתים רבים . . . בית בבית). The pericope 10 1-4a, if a part of the chain[23], parallels these to some extent and shows considerable poetical polish. The *Ankündigung* is not explicit, however, but refracted in a question reminiscent of Am 5 18-20 and 6 1f. Where the woe is sufficiently full to allow any conclusion (verses 8f. 11ff.), the speaker is the prophet, not the Lord. The remaining woes of this chain not only lack any close adaptation to the *Gerichtsrede*, but show varying degrees of fullness[24].

In contrast to their heterogeneity in form these woes are marked by a noteworthy unity of content, which has been described well by O. Kaiser:

> In den sieben Weherufen wendet sich der Prophet gegen die allgemeine Auflösung der geheiligten Ordnungen Israels durch gewissenlose Kapitalisten, genußsüchtige Schlemmer, bewußte und spottende Übertreter der Gottesgebote, Verkehrer der Wahrheit und des Rechtes. Sie fügen sich zu einem derartig geschlossenen Gesamtbild zusammen, daß es nicht unwahrscheinlich ist, daß sie auch von vornherein von Jesaja als Einheit gedacht und vorgetragen worden sind.[25]

This unity of content is striking. We might summarize it even more tersely: These woes are directed against those who in their self-reliant "secularism" destroy the people of God[26]. What does the *hôy*,

---

[23] Final certainty concerning the original attachement of the woe of 10 1-4 is impossible. Kaiser's categorical assertion "Fest steht aber, daß 5 8-24 und 10 1-4a literarisch ursprünglich zusammengehörten" (Jesaja 50f.) is countered by detailed argumentation to the contrary in two recent studies (R. Fey, Amos und Jesaja, 83—104, especially 83—87; H. Donner, Israel unter den Völkern, 1964, 66—75). Both Fey and Donner take 10 1-4 to be the fourth stanza of a poem addressed to the reduced Northern Kingdom before 722 B. C. (and after 733 B. C.; Donner), a poem consisting of 9 7 to 10 4, plus 5 25-29. As to content and catch-word association (*hôy*) the former conclusion is inviting. On the other hand, the arguments for the place of 10 1-4 in the poem just outlined are too strong to be disregarded. One is tempted to posit the incorporation of a *hôy* from the chain 5 8-24—or an unattached *hôy* of the same brand—into the poem 9 7—10 4 5 25-29. However, the closeness of the oracle to the chain of chapter 5 may be due to a deeper unity which pervades the proclamation of Isaiah. We will discuss 10 1-4 separately from 5 8-24, assuming that its place within the poem mentioned is at least very fitting, if not undisputedly original. At the same time, everything said about the woes 5 8-24 could be applied fittingly to this woe also, as it shares in the general character of the earlier Isaianic woes against Israel.

[24] We agree fully with Wildberger (Jesaja 182) when he says: "Die Weherufe von 20 und 21 sind demnach durchaus intakt und nicht als Fragmente zu beurteilen."

[25] Kaiser, Jesaja, 56.

[26] Wildberger (Jesaja 175—202) shows throughout his discussion how these woes are to be understood on the basis of Israel's covenant relationship to Yahweh, and the social order grounded in it. This does not preclude the recognition of wisdom terminology or concerns here and there; such features must be understood in their specific function within the proclamation of Isaiah, however.

cast at them, mean? Where an *Ankündigung* is present or implied, it points to a reversal of fate (8-10. 11-13). On the whole, we appear to have little more than a series of rather general injunctions against vaguely specified evil.

It is this relative contextlessness which has given fuel to the claim of a wisdom origin for *hôy*. Even the advocates of that claim would not hold, however, that Isaiah was a wisdom teacher who dispensed instruction to the young towards their growth in righteousness. The question concerning the place of these woes within the prophetic proclamation of Isaiah is unavoidable. For its answer we are dependent on the possibility of establishing a relationship between these woes and other prophetic woes which stand less isolated[27].

Two themes draw attention. First, feasting and carousing is the basis of the *hôy* in verses 11-13 (17 ?)[28] and in 22, feasting that will turn into its opposite, deathly hunger and thirst in exile. This pattern is precisely that which we recognized as the Day of the Lord-setting in Amos[29]. In fact, the similarity between Is 5 11-13 and Am 6 1-7 is so striking that Fey has argued rather convincingly for an actual literary dependence of Isaiah on Amos[30].

The second theme is expressed in Is 5 12b and 19: *Hôy* is pronounced over those who fail to recognize the "signs of the times"[31] and therefore

---

[27] When we speak of these woes as "isolated," we presuppose, with most recent commentators, that they are not an original part of the preceding Song of the Vineyard (5 1-7) or the following poem (5 25ff.). We have discussed the latter elsewhere. Verse 24b is generally recognized as a concluding subscript to the whole series of woes. The association of the woes with the materials collected in Is 2—5 is not without significance, however. These materials show a thematic relatedness, and while it cannot be our task here to discuss their originality and composition, the association of the woes with such (genuinely Isaianic) passages as the description of Yahweh's day against the haughty (2 12-17) or the poetic indictment of the Song of the Vineyard against covenant breakers (5 1-7) does point to that realm of Isaianic proclamation within which they are at home.

[28] The place of verse 17 is uncertain. Scott (The Interpreter's Bible V 201) sees in it the continuation of verse 13. Wildberger (Jesaja 181. 189f.) combines verses 14 and 17 into a fragmentary woe.   [29] See above, 41ff., especially 44f.

[30] Fey, Amos und Jesaja, 7—17. Note also the helpful discussion of the difference between the preoccupation of wisdom with the topic "wine" (Prov 23 29-35) and the prophetic concern with that subject (8—10).

[31] The specific meaning of מעשה ידיו פעל יהוה (verse 12), מעשהו, עצת קדוש (verse 19) and related terms in the theology of Isaiah is the subject of an excursus by Wildberger (Jesaja 188f.). He makes clear that reference here is to the plan of Yahweh within present events, in contrast to the use of these terms (in the plural!) in the Psalter where they point back to the *magnalia dei* in the past. He inquires concerning their origin and considers for a moment the possibility of a Holy War background, but rejects it abruptly and without reason: "Aus welchem Bereich hat sie Jesaja

live in imagined security while the Lord's history is already far advanced towards that catastrophe—an historical catastrophe (verse 13) —which will bring their destruction. Again we are in the orbit of the theology of Amos, a theology shared more explicitly by Isaiah in the poem 9 7—10 4 5 26-29. We will discuss it more fully in that connection[32]; suffice it to say here that the presence of this theme is further evidence that the woes of Is 5 8-24 can be visualized well within a pattern of proclamation essentially the same as that which forms the setting for the woes of Amos.

That this proclamation of the Lord's history with his covenant-breaking people can also be couched in imagery which remains non-specifying and general is illustrated by Am 5 18-20 and need not, therefore, surprise us in Is 5 20-23. To see wisdom here is not necessary[33]. Finally, the closeness of Is 5 8-10 to Am 5 11-12a may serve as a further tie between the woes of Is 5 and the place of the woes worked out for those of Amos[34].

The elements of funerary lament are nowhere evident in Is 5 8-24, nor is there any indication, apart from the possible implication of *hôy* itself, that Isaiah speaks in proleptic mourning. References to death, or death imagery appear marginally in the cliché of 5 9b and in 5 13 (כבודו מת רעב)[35]; the theme of "death" for "death," in a more general sense, permeates the whole passage, however.

übernommen? Er steht in der Tradition des heiligen Krieges. Aber von dorther stammen die Begriffe nicht" (189). Instead, he argues for a background in the wisdom of the king, using 28 23-29 as link in the argument. Such an interpretation falls before the cogent presentation of von Rad (Theologie des Alten Testament II 168 —170): To behold the work of the Lord is the posture of those who — in Isaiah's Holy War theology — recognize the sovereign Lord at work to execute his plan revealed to the prophet in the Heavenly Council, — a plan in which the faithful must stand aside in quietness and trust. Wildberger also acknowledges von Rad's thesis (Jesaja 201), but apparently does not see it in its whole Holy War-Day of the Lord panorama.   [32] See below, 53 ff., n. 37.

[33] Fey (Amos und Jesaja 57 ff.) argues for a shaping influence of Amos on Is 5 20. 23 also.

[34] Fey (ibid. 59 ff.) claims dependence again. This may be the place to fortify our use of Fey's results against any misunderstanding. Fey's thesis seems to demonstrate convincingly that Isaiah knew a number of Amos' oracles and used them for his own purposes (against Wolff's critique in: Amos' geistige Heimat 55—58). Our argumentation, however, is not dependent on Fey's thesis; it does not demand proof of dependence, but merely claims a function for the somewhat contextless *hôy's* of Is 5 which is similar to that of the *hôy*-words of Amos. A common rootedness of the two prophets in the same historical-theological soil would be sufficient to account for this.

[35] With LXX, Syriac, Targum, though the MT reading is also possible and perhaps the *lectio difficilior*, unless one adopt מזה or מזי on the basis of Dt 32 24, though without manuscript support (BHmg; Wildberger, Jesaja, 177).

The question whether the prophet uses *hôy* with awareness of its mourning background cannot, therefore, be answered on the basis of this section. The understanding of these *hôy*-words, in this respect, remains completely dependent on one's understanding of *hôy* gained from other contexts. We believe to have shown, however, that it is not necessary to interpret these woes as general wisdom admonitions outside of any specific place in God's history with his people, but that, instead, there are weighty indications that a theological context similar to that of Amos' proclamation of the Day of the Lord may have been the setting of these woes.

The woe of 10 1-4 has already been discussed in part[36]. In the context of 9 7—10 4 5 25-29 it is addressed to the Northern Kingdom shortly before 722 B. C. This lengthy poem places its addressees into a moment in history held in tension between disasters of the past which have not yet been understood by Israel as to their divine purpose, and events to come which will be inescapably clear to Israel and final in their fierceness. This tension is upheld in the repeated refrain "For all this his anger is not turned away and his hand is stretched out still" (9 11.16.20 10 4 5 25). It is against those who, in their mistaken security, continue to destroy "my people" (10 2) through social injustice, that the *hôy* of 10 1 is hurled in anticipation of the יום פקדה (10 3), which will be the work of Yaweh himself (5 25) through his agent called from afar (5 26 10 3) and from which there will be no escape[37].

Fey has worked out convincingly the parallelism of this *Geschichtsdeutung* to that of Am 4 6-12a[38]. In his own summary:

Allein die Tatsache, daß beide Propheten einen Geschichtsrückblick in Form eines Kehrversgedichts bieten, dabei ausschließlich ergangene Gerichte, keine Heilstaten Jahwes erwähnen und das Ganze mit einer Gerichtsankündigung, die alles vorangegangene Unheil überbietet, abschließen, ist so merkwürdig, daß eine unbeeinflußte Entstehung bei Jesaja von vornherein alle Wahrscheinlichkeit gegen sich hat. Daß dieses Jesajagedicht (wie 28 1-4) zudem ausdrücklich an das Nordreich gerichtet ist (7),

---

[36] See above, 50 and n. 23. For details of textual and formal analysis see the sources cited there.

[37] It is this schema which Wildberger (Jesaja 208) has missed when he objects to the sequence 9 7-20 10 1-4 on the basis that 9 7-20 speaks about divine judgements already past, while the woe of 10 1-4 looks toward future happenings. Understood in the tension between past and future, as described, 10 1-4 continues 9 7-20 suitably, while the reasons given for its original unity with and later detachment from 5 8-24 bear the marks of arbitrariness. Even such a detachment — if it should have been the case, which is not altogether impossible — were best motivated precisely by the suitability of the incorporation of the woe into the poem beginning with 9 7.

[38] Even if one were hesitant to follow Fey in his broad claims for actual dependence of Isaiah on Amos (cf. above, 52, n. 34), one can hardly escape the conclusion that the two prophets share here the same panoramic view of history from the same vantage point.

dem auch der Amosspruch galt (4 12a), daß also der Jerusalemer Prophet sein opus proprium verläßt und sich an Menschen wendet (8), denen Amos, nicht er selbst, gegenüberstand, verstärkt den Eindruck, daß Jesaja sich hier wieder bewußt in Amos Fußstapfen stellt.[39]

For our investigation it is of further importance, that an interpretation of history, a *Geschichtsdeutung* with very similar, though not identical stages is carried forward by the five visions of Amos (7 1-3.4-6.7-9 8 1-3 9 1-4): At first doom is averted (7 1-3. 4-6); then the Lord will "never again pass by" his people (7 7-9 8 1-3) until he is fully recognized as the one who brings the punishment and from whom there is no escape (9 1-4; cf. Is 10 3). We have already discussed the place of *hôy* in the pattern of the approaching Day in Amos[40], and we now recognize it in an identical function in a very similar pattern in the Isaiah-poem under discussion.

IV. Isaiah: The Remaining Woes

The second series of Isaianic *hôy*-words consists of 28 1 29 1 29 15 30 1 and 31 1, passages from the later ministry of Isaiah, except 28 1-4, a passage concerning the end of the Northern Kingdom, as perhaps, 10 5ff. and 17 12-14, while 18 1-6 may belong to the later Assyrian crisis[41].

In spite of some dissolution of formal terseness 28 1-4 is quite recognizable as a literary unit dominated by "reversal of imagery". The "proud crown" (עטרת גאות) and "fading flower" (ציץ נבל)—perhaps "proud wreath"[42]—are torn down, trodden under foot and consumed. The characteristic marks of the *Gerichtsrede* are absent. While punishment is to come upon the haughty, the formal structure is determined by this "reversal of imagery", rather than the balance of *Begründung* and *Ankündigung*. The pericope is not divine speech. The image presents a sharp and unexpected contrast of fate brought about by the Lord's own agent who turns the security of exaltation and feasting into utter ruin. Procksch thinks of the "proud crown" as the city walls of Samaria[43], though one could also consider it a more general image to characterize the upper classes who are intoxicated by their

---

[39] Fey, Amos und Jesaja, 88f.
[40] See above, 44f.
[41] The Isaiah-passages pertaining to the Assyrian crisis of the latter eighth century B. C. have been discussed recently in H. Donner, Israel unter den Völkern, 1964, and B. S. Childs, Isaiah and the Assyrian Crisis, 1967.
[42] Thus O. Procksch, Jesaja I, 1930, ad locum.
[43] Ibid.

luxury and power. The agent of the Lord will be Assyria. The events still lie in the future. Terminology of death and mourning is absent, unless the reversal of feasting into its opposite, a theme that character-izes other *hôy*-passages[44], indirectly implies a situation of mourning. While directed at men of the Northern Kingdom, this woe conforms fully to the characterization given to the woes of Is 5 8-24, except that the sweeping onslaught of the Lord's campaign against Israel —through his agent—is made explicit. Verses 5-6 are probably second-ary[45], but the editor's understanding of verses 1-4 as pertaining to "that day" is perfectly correct.

The oracle against Jerusalem-Ariel, Is 29 1-4. 5c-6, abounds in difficulties[46]. A rather unbalanced *Gerichtswort* could be discerned, with a shorter *Begründung* (verses 1-2) and a longer *Ankündigung* (verses 3-4. 5c-6), the latter in the form of divine speech. More prominent, however, is the "reversal of imagery", both in the repetition of the name Ariel in the enigmatic statement "and she shall be to me like an Ariel" (verse 2) and in the play on חנה in verse 1a and verse 3a. As, in addition, no messenger formula or *lākēn* or *kî* is present, a certain independence towards the *Gerichtsrede* is preserved.

The security of the city of David with its sacral tradition and reassuring festival calendar will be reversed into lamentation and death by the onslaught of the Divine Warrior himself[47]. The "before-after" tension and the movement from feasting to mourning and to Sheol-imagery (verse 4) are typical of the funerary lament. If one adds to

---

[44] Cf. our discussion of this pattern above, 41ff., in connection with Amos.

[45] Against Donner, Israel, 75f.

[46] For the reasons for this delimitation, see Childs (Isaiah 53—57), who discerns two layers: "The primary oracle (verses 1-4. 5c-6) was an invective-threat directed against Jerusalem. A secondary level (5a. b. 6) transformed the oracle into a promise by adding a word of threat to the nations which was drawn from the language of the older Zion tradition" (57). This analysis is not uncontested; Donner (Israel 154f.), for ex-ample, denies any connection of verses 5f. with verses 1-4. Both Scott (The Inter-preter's Bible V 322f.) and von Rad (Theologie II 165) reach conclusions very similar to those of Childs. Some uncertainty cannot be excluded; it is possible that an originally compact and balanced woe against Ariel, verses 1-4, was (fittingly) expanded in verses 5c-6, or that a later word of promise was added to the earlier woe (cf. Is 28 5-6).

[47] The reference to David is difficult, but that some reversal from a positively assessed past to a condemned present is involved cannot be questioned. A play on the range of meaning of חנה seems involved: Formerly Ariel was the city where David "pitched camp" (with reference to the end of the wanderings of Israel and the ark ?!); now the Lord will encamp (in the sense of siege) against her. If one accepts כְּדָוִד (with LXX) for כַדּוּר (verse 3), the accent shifts somewhat: David's campaign (חנה now with reference to siege here, too) — a divinely blessed act in Israel's *Heilsgeschichte* — is contrasted to the Lord's Holy War against Jerusalem.

this the fact that *hôy* is followed by a twice-repeated name, it becomes more than likely that this *Gerichtsrede* has been shaped in the image of the funerary lament. The setting of *hôy* in the Holy War-Day of the Lord pattern, by now familiar to us, is unmistakable in this pericope.

Is 29 15-16 shows a fusion of *hôy* with a proverb, perhaps evoked by verse 14. The employment of wisdom idiom is not in itself un-Isaianic[48], and the accusation of reversing the true values stands at the centre of Isaiah's proclamation[49]. To see here an expression of the true wisdom character of *hôy*, however, would be overdemanding the evidence. A comparison of this passage with Is 45 9f. shows how fluctuating the relation of the *hôy* to such following proverbs is[50]. In these passages the question without *hôy* could well be the original (wisdom) saying, as Is 29 15 may suggest, analogous to such questions as Is 10 15. The only thing that can be said in connection with our study is that *hôy* is again directed at those who act self-reliantly.

Is 30 1-5 and 31 1-3 arise out of the same political situation and are largely parallel. 30 1-5 presents itself as a *Gerichtsrede* as completely as any *hôy*-pericope in Isaiah. Its content is lack of reliance on the Lord, which leads to a reversal of fate, carried into the very terminology again (verse 2b and verse 3). The oracle is divine speech throughout, however.

The woe of 31 1-3, though attaching the very same characterization to the addressees, shows none of the specific marks of *Gerichtsrede*, nor does it claim to be divine speech. Upon exclusion of verse 2[51], a closely knit woe, reminiscent in form of Am 5 18-20 or Is 28 1-4, results, a woe more descriptive and predictive than condemnatory. No mourning terminology or context appears in the two words just discussed. The *hôy* in each case is directed against the self-reliance of the haughty who fail to recognize God's direction of history and seek to direct the affairs of Judah autonomous of him, a situation reminiscent of Is 5 12b. 19[52].

It is generally held that Is 1 4-9 belongs to the Assyrian crisis of Isaiah's latter days also. In contrast to the other woes of Isaiah, this passage does not look into the future but laments what has already taken place. Commentators agree on the fact that we have here a mourning lamentation, even though the technical vocabulary of that genre, with the exception of *hôy*, is not present. It is prophetic, not divine speech. The addressing of the whole nation contrasts with

---

[48] Cf. J. Fichtner, Jesaja unter den Weisen, ThLZ 74 (1949), 75ff.

[49] J. Fichtner, Die Umkehrung.

[50] Cf. Westermann, Das Buch Jesaja, Kapitel 40—66, 1966, 135.

[51] Following Donner (Israel 135ff.) and Childs (Isaiah 33—35); Childs calls the verse a hymnic inclusion.

[52] Cf. our discussion of these verses, above, 51f.

the more selective definition of the addressee in *hôy*-words, when directed at Israelite groups, though it corresponds to those directed at foreign nations (Is 10 5). This is in keeping with Fohrer's analysis of Is 1 as a summary of the prophet's message[53]. The passage shares with the majority of Isaianic (and other) woes its thrust against self-willed, stubborn covenant breakers[54]. It differs from the majority of them in its greater closeness to funerary lament, due, no doubt, to its pronouncement after the Assyrian onslaught of 701 B. C. In other words, this woe laments *post factu* what the other woes have warningly and threateningly bewailed in advance. That the Assyrian onslaught is seen here as Yahweh's Holy War against Israel has been demonstrated by Wildberger through an analysis of Holy War terminology in verses 7-9[55].

The character of funerary lament is evident even more clearly in 1 21-26, a passage held by many to belong to the time of the Assyrian crisis also, though it may well be earlier[56]. We have already cited this pericope as one of our primary pieces of evidence for the preservation of *hôy* in the lamentation-vengeance sequence[57]. Fohrer has characterized it succinctly:

> Motive des Leichenliedes sind das einleitende "ach" [איכה] und die Klage in v. 21a, der Preis der früheren Tugenden und Eigenschaften und der Vergleich mit dem jetzigen Verfall in v. 21b-22, die Rachedrohung gegen die Mörder in v. 24-25 und die Tröstung in v. 26.[58]

---

[53] G. Fohrer, Jesaja 1 als Zusammenfassung der Verkündung Jesajas, ZAW 74 (1962), 251—268.

[54] The background of this passage in covenant theology has been worked out well by Wildberger (Jesaja 18—31). A thematic relationship to the *rîb* of 1 2-3 is thus created, though an original unity of composition is unlikely. (See Wildberger ibid. 9; Fohrer, Jesaja 1 als Zusammenfassung, 254f.).

[55] Wildberger, Jesaja, 26—31. To avoid misunderstanding, it should be said that the sweeping onslaught of the Divine Warrior, with its Holy War-Day of the Lord terminology, should not be understood as a dot on the time-line, but as a quality or category of Divine activity in history, a quality in which various concrete historical events participate more or less fully. Thus Is 1 4-9 can lament a nation already struck by the impact of the Lord's war, and at the same time serve the obvious purpose of calling to repentance, lest it come. In Christian theology the coming of the Kingdom forms the parallel yet further developed doctrine.

[56] Ibid. 58. Wildberger's reminder that no specific danger or war is explicitly mentioned, that the accusation is directed at internal decay, and that the passage is close to others (3 12-15 5 22-24 10 1-4) from Isaiah's earlier years, can hardly be discounted. If we discuss this woe at this point in our study, we do so largely out of favourable disposition towards Fohrer's view of Isaiah 1 as a summary of the message of Isaiah (to Jerusalem and Judah, we might add; chapter 1 does not include words addressed to foreign nations).   [57] See above, 33.

[58] G. Fohrer, Das Buch Jesaja, 1960, 45, n. 18. His last reference to verse 26 as a consolation lends itself to misunderstanding, however. In Jesaja 1 als Zusammen-

In its present form a *Gerichtsrede*, consisting of *Begründung* (verses 21-23) and *Ankündigung* (verses 24-26) is usually assumed by commentators, the former being prophetic, and the latter divine speech. The formula of verse 24a is somewhat unusual however[59], and the real cohesion of the pericope is again the reversal of imagery, bracketed by the opening and closing reference to the "faithful city"[60]. The conscious employment of *hôy* in a uniform literary unit which moves from lamentation to vengeance is beyond doubt[61]. The vengeance will be performed by the Lord and will—implicitly, though nowhere stated directly—exist of the coming of his Day, as Wild-

---

fassung (265—267) he becomes more specific: By the cleansing of Jerusalem from the corrupt upper classes the rest of the people can be restored. (Cf. our discussion of Mic 2 1-5, below 62). For the features of the funerary lament in this segment see also especially Jahnow, Das hebräische Leichenlied, 254f.

[59] That the individual elements of this unusual chain are Isaianic has been shown in detail by Wildberger (Jesaja 62—64), and the text is well attested. It is not secondary expansion with which we are dealing here, but rather a conscious highlighting of the contrast of those who act in utter disrespect of the (Davidic tradition of) the covenant obligations, and the stepping in of the Lord as his own avenger as well as the avenger of the downtrodden. The gathering of Isaianic epithets supports Fohrer's thesis concerning the summary character of Isaiah 1.

[60] The reversal has been characterized succinctly by Fey (Amos und Jesaja 64): "Prophetenrede 21-23 und Gotteswort 24b-26 sind in genauer chiastischer Entsprechung aufeinander bezogen: es korrespondieren 21a und 26b, 21b und 26a, 22 und 25, 23 und 24b."

[61] When interpreters speak of formal adaptations, tensions, fusions, etc., this is correct in so far as a particular form of the funerary lament has been applied to a situation where the guilt is not individual but corporate and consists of "murder" (of the downtrodden through the unfaithfulness to covenant justice on the part of the leaders) in a derived sense. It is not correct if it means that a beginning along the lines of funerary lament (verses 21-23) has been extended, due to prophetic usage, into a prophetic "threat" (*Drohwort*) (Fey, Amos und Jesaja, 65; Fohrer, Jesaja, I 46; even Jahnow, Das hebräische Leichenlied, 255, where she says: "schon im v. 23 gleitet die Qina in eine prophetische Scheltrede über"). Here the transition from lament to vengeance, as a frequent version of funerary lamentation (see above, 27ff.), described clearly by Jahnow (54f. 88f. etc.) in other connections, has gone unrecognized. The closeness of this possibility in funerary lamentation to the prophetic sequence of *Begründung-Ankündigung* must have been a significant factor in the selection of *hôy* by the prophets for their purposes. (See below, 81ff.).

This lamentation-vengeance background leads us to wonder whether the general tendency to excise וְעַתָּה מְרַצְּחִים (verse 21c) for metrical reasons is well considered, for this phrase not only emphasizes the "then-now" theme of funerary lament, but summarizes and makes explicit the blood-guilt against which the avenger sets out. Would it not be as appropriate to see one of the first two cola of the verse as having been attracted into the verse by the other? If 21c were really a gloss, however, it must have been added by one who knew the background of such speech and reached into its repertoire for a fitting term (against Fey, Amos und Jesaja, 64).

berger points out, but a day inverted against Jerusalem instead of the
foreign nations[62].

The remaining three Isaianic woes (10 5 17 12 18 1) are directed
against foreign nations. The scope of 10 5ff. is not easily determined,
but includes at least verse 15[63]. The pericope is now secondarily
attached to 10 1-4, but is a self-contained unit. A *Gerichtsrede*-pattern
can be imposed superficially only, if one considers verses 16-19 to be
the *Ankündigung*[64]. Verses 5-15 consist of four formal units: the woe-
oracle in the narrower sense, verses 5-7, followed by two speeches of
Assyria, verses 8-11 and verses 13-14, separated by a prose summary,
verse 12, and followed by a proverbial question, verse 15, a question,
however, that returns to the figure of the rod, introduced in verse 5,
thus rounding out verses 5-15 into a formally marked unit. The woe is
spoken by the Lord in the first person and is directly addressed. The
time seems to be after 717 B. C.[65]. The thrust of the passage is clear
and uniform and is well captured by the interplay of imagery between
verses 5 and 15. It is the rebellion of the instrument in its self-styled
sovereignty against the sovereignty of the Lord. The terminology of
mourning is nowhere in evidence.

In Is 17 12-14 the *hôy* has lost its historical contours as the nations
and the chaos waters thunder (against Mount Zion), but are rebuked
and flee[66]. Von Rad sees here a veritable model of the old Zion tradi-

---

[62] An appraisal of the use of קנא and נחם leads Wildberger to say, "Das heißt, Jesaja
kündet hier faktisch, wie es in 2 12 expressis verbis geschieht, einen Jahwetag an, nur
daß die Feinde Jahwes, an denen er sich rächen wird, die Jerusalemer sind!"
(Jesaja 64 f.).

[63] Thus Kaiser (Jesaja 111—115) and Childs (Isaiah 39—44). That several small forms
are employed goes without saying; the question is, to what extent the composite
oracle is a composition of the prophet himself. Nothing speaks against Isaianic origin
of verses 5-15, the generally recognized glosses verse 10 and verse 12 excepted. Our
formal outline follows Childs, with the exception of his retention of verse 12 as original.
It is probably an interpolation, though a very appropriate and perceptive one, and
quite possibly Isaianic (cf. von Rad, Theologie, II 170).

[64] For a full listing of reasons against this, see Kaiser, Jesaja, 115—117. Donner (Israel
145) thinks that a *Drohwort* has been replaced by the present verses 16-19. However,
the vocabulary of these verses is admittedly Isaianic (which Kaiser takes as a symptom
of a learned concoction by someone familiar with Isaiah's words). Kaiser's rejection
is, perhaps, influenced too strongly by his understanding of the scene as a "ruhendes
Landschaftsbild," in contrast to the "beweglichen Assyrerheer" of verses 5-15. If the
fire-imagery of these verses is related to Holy War, however, rather than to actual
fire or to draught, this contrast disappears. (Cf. also von Rad, Theologie, II 169f.).

[65] This widely held dating is based on the reference to Carchemish (verse 9), which was
incorporated into the Assyrian Empire by Sargon II in 717 B. C. (Cf. Kaiser, Jesaja,
112).

[66] The problems raised by this passage are summarized by Childs, Isaiah, 50—53.

tion so prominent in Isaiah and relates it to Yahweh's Holy War
against the nations, in the face of which those who believe must only
be still[67]. The oracle is not easily classified formally, nor is its relation
to its context clear; it is certainly not a *Gerichtsrede*. Its speaker
cannot be determined. For our purposes we note the employment of
hôy in a word announcing the "Day of the Lord" against the nations.

Is 18 1-6 has been interpreted variously, but basic to all interpretations is the understanding of מלאכים (verse 2) as standing in
parallelism to צירים, so that the imperative לכו is addressed to the
Ethiopic messengers[68]. The difficulties of interpretation thus evoked
are well illustrated by Donner's[69] attempt to visualize the situation:
The oracle must have been translated (!) to the Ethiopic messengers
in the streets of Jerusalem. But since no threat against Ethiopia
follows, according to Donner, the *hôy* could not have meant "woe,"
but must have consisted of a "langgezogenen Ruf . . ., mit dem Jesaja
die Aufmerksamkeit seiner Zuhörer auf sich lenken wollte". Even
then, Donner concludes, the whole thing could not have made much
sense to these worshippers of Amun of Thebes! We agree; a radically
different understanding is necessary.

We would suggest that Ez 30 9—secondary in that context and
probably fashioned on Is 18 2[70]—points the way to a more tenable
understanding of our oracle: The *hôy* is directed against Ethiopia,
whose envoys have come to Jerusalem. Over against these political
manoevers, the prophet sees the Lord take counter-measures in his
Divine Council by sending his own messengers[71]. The reversal of
imagery, associated so frequently with *hôy*, is evident again: The
Ethiopic צירים are countered by the Lord's מלאכים. The latter are
sent to Assyria (cf. Is 5 26)[72]. The description of verse 2 authenticates
the nation addressed here as the agent of punishment (cf. Is 5 26
Hab 1 6ff.). But as the Lord's punishment is never petty warfare,

---

[67] Von Rad, Theologie, II 162—175.

[68] Thus recently again Childs, Isaiah, 44—46, and Donner, Israel, 121—126.

[69] Ibid. 124.

[70] See W. Zimmerli, Ezechiel, 1957—, ad locum. Messengers in ships (בצים, בציים,
MT, Vulgate) does not make sense there; it shows that the verse was either fashioned
on Is 18 2, or, more likely (since Is 18 2 uses different terms for the seafaring messengers), that it was revised from an original אצים (LXX, Syriac) in the light of Is 18 2.
Both possibilities would uphold our interpretation. As the whole verse 9 a represents
a series of clichés, it cannot be decided whether מלפני is a (correct) secondary addition
e sensu in MT, or an haplography in LXX.

[71] See F. M. Cross. The Council of Yahweh in Second Isaiah, JNES 12 (1953), 274—277.

[72] The reference to Ethiopic messengers is sufficiently unspecific to make it impossible
to decide whether the political context is the plotting agains Assyria which preceded
711 B. C. (cf. ch. 20), as Scott (The Interpreter's Bible V 276) would have it, or shortly
after 705 B. C., with Donner (Israel 120f).

it is a holocaust involving his adversaries far and wide; the whole world (verse 3) is implicated (cf. 14 26). The *hôy* against Ethiopia/ Egypt, then, introduces the announcement of the Lord's Day (cf. Ez 30 9)[73].

V. The Isaianic Woes: Preliminary Conclusions

Our survey of Isaianic woes permits certain preliminary conclusions. Where the context offers adequate evidence, there is no doubt that *hôy* is pronounced within an interpretation of an historical moment (101-4 281-4 291-4 301-5 311-3 14-9 1 21-26 105-15 181-6), and even where contextual evidence is sparse, the same conclusion seems indicated and plausible (5 8-24 29 15-16 17 12-14). At no point does it become necessary, or even at all inviting, to understand the immediate context of *hôy* as originally independent of its present historical nexus and as sapiential in character.

The moments of history which evoke Isaiah's *hôy*-pronouncements combine to project a situation of considerable uniformity: The *hôy* is almost invariably directed at addressees who act in self-reliant independence of Yahweh. These are confronted—whether threateningly or mournfully—with the certainty that the Lord will bring low their haughty independence, usually by a reversal of their present condition into its opposite, a reversal that is carried into the words and images employed. This is true whether the addressee is a part of God's people Israel (14-9 1 21-26 5 8-24 101-4 281-4 291-4 29 15-16 301-5 311-3) or a foreign nation (105-15 17 12-14 18 1-6); a differentation between the function of *hôy* on the basis of its addressee seems unwarranted. The place of this historical situation within the panorama of the Lord's Holy War against his enemies to bring in his Day, as noted in connection with the woes of Amos, is explicitly indicated for many Isaianic *hôy*-pericopes (10 1-4 28 1-4 29 1-4 1 21-26 17 12-14 18 1-6), and quite appropriate and plausible for others (5 8-24 29 15-16 30 1-5 31 1-3 10 5-15, cf. also 1 4-9). Mourning terminology and imagery is absent from the greater number of Isaianic woes, but its presence in 29 1-4 1 4-9 and 1 21-26 assures Isaiah's consciousness of the background of *hôy* in funerary lament. Its place in the historic panorama under discussion has been shown earlier. The characterization of *hôy*-words as expressing primarily a concern for social justice[74] is possible only if one selects a limited number of *hôy*-words as the basis of characterization[75]. To be sure, *hôy*

---

[73] In Ez 30 9 the ביום ההוא is appropriately particularized to ביום מצרים.

[74] Cf. Westermann, Grundformen, 139; Gerstenberger, The Woe Oracles, 225 f.

[75] See above, 3 f., 19 f.

is frequently addressed to those who transgress in that area, but such infringement is lifted out as one of the symptoms of rebellious covenant breaking and forms a sub-theme under the overarching concern just outlined[76].

In contrast to this persistently uniform context of the *hôy*-pericopes their formal features show a remarkable lack of uniformity. Most of them resemble the structure of the prophetic *Gerichtsrede* only superficially, so that one best understands that resemblance as being due to the influence of the prophetic context. On the other hand, the variant features distinguishing the woes from the *Gerichtsrede* are not sufficiently constant to allow one to posit an earlier, distinctly coined *hôy*-form, supposedly adapted later to prophetic speech. The generally noticed participle after *hôy* is by no means a constant; a noun of general scope (1 4 5 21 5 22 17 2 18 1 30 1), or a proper noun (10 5 29 1) can describe the adressee equally well, and that within the usage just outlined. A finite verb follows in 1 24. Once one participle is chosen, a second one in a parallel colon will, of course, be easily attracted, though not necessarily. One gains the distinct impression that it is only the *fact* of an address after *hôy*, but not the nature of that address, which is a stable feature. If this is so, one can conclude at least for Isaiah that the search for a formula of some length, and characteristic features beyond *hôy* plus address, is a methodological error. Isaiah seems to have borrowed from the realm of mourning[77] merely this kernel[78] and to have used it for the message characterized above, a message completely consonant with his central proclamation[79]. That certain trends, such as the use of the participle, gain some prominence in the prophetic use of *hôy* is true, but it were better to see in them developments *within* prophecy, called forth by the demands of use and context, than to suppose them to be hallmarks of an earlier genre entering prophecy from another realm.

VI. Micah 2 1-5

The *hôy*-pericope Mic 2 1-5 has internal cohesion and presents itself as prophetic *Gerichtsrede*, opening with a *Begründung* (verses 1-2) consisting of a *hôy* followed by participial clauses, which are then

---

[76] As the covenant stipulations are a frequent concern of the sapiential instruction in the clan (*Sippenethos*) also, there is a meeting of themes here, but this cannot be the basis on which to claim, with Gerstenberger and others, a sapiential origin for *hôy*.

[77] For an assessment of the relation to Amos, see below, 84ff.

[78] We recall that "alas" plus addressee ("Alas, brother!", etc.) is the basic mourning cry.

[79] Particularly relevant here are the dicussions by J. Fichtner (Die „Umkehrung" . . .) and G. von Rad (Theologie II 154—181, especially 162ff.).

expanded. A messenger formula makes the transition to the *Ankündigung* (verses 3-5)[80]. The two parts are held together by reversal of imagery also: Against the devisers of wickedness (חשבי־און) and workers of evil (פעלי רע) Yahweh will now be a deviser of evil (חשב רעה).

The guilt of the accused consists of ruthless acquisition of the covenant portion (נחלה) of the poor man, reminiscent of Ahab's acquisition of Naboth's vineyard (I Kings 21), and the punishment, though vaguely alluded to, appears to be defeat and the loss of their lands (verse 3). This theme is continued in the broken text of verse 4, as well as in verse 5. Verse 4[81], by designation a taunt-song[82], and as to form and content a taunting lamentation, specifies the general

---

[80] As to the delimitation of the pericope we agree with A. Alt (Micha 2 1-5. ΓΗΣ ANA-ΔAΣΜΟΣ in Juda, Kleine Schriften, III 1959, 372—381), who points out the return in verses 4-5 to the concerns raised in verses 1-2 (376 f.). The literary seams in the pericope are taken by Alt (with Duhm) as marks of a three-stanza poem (verses 1-2. 3. 4-5). We would add that verses 3-4 have now been fused into an *Ankündigung*, perhaps through insertion of the messenger-formula at the beginning of verse 3. The precise literary history of the pericope is beyond reconstruction, but its present cohesion seems assured. LXX has εγένοντο (= היו) for *hôy*, but all interpreters agree that MT is original.

[81] This verse has been considered to be a fragment of a funerary lament (Robinson, Die Zwölf Kleinen Propheten, 134). It certainly has the marks of that genre, but its content is so specifically tailored to verses 1-2 that Micah himself must have resorted to that form of speech.

The text is hopelessly corrupt. נהיה should be deleted, with LXX and Targum. The remaining difficulties do not affect our inquiry, except one: LXX renders לי איך ימיש as καὶ οὐκ ἦν ὁ κωλύσων αὐτόν (ואין משיב). This reading seems to have been influenced by verse 5. Although the verse could be characterized as a נהי even without איך, its alteration to אין appears to be an unwarranted *lectio facilior*. Note the designation משל for Is 14 4ff., a taunting funerary lament beginning איך (verse 4), repeated again later (verse 12)! The participle is modelled after that of verse 5; its object αὐτόν seems to refer to an agent not named in the series of Greek passives, but implied in the third-person active speech of MT, which appropriately contrasts with the first person of MT. This strengthens the impression that LXX offers a form-critically insensitive facilitating reading.

[82] The area of meaning covered by the term משל has been explored by A. R. Johnson (מָשָׁל, Wisdom in Israel and in the Ancient Near East, 162-169). For our purposes two observations are important: First, the term is by no means limited to wisdom speech, but contains the possibility of approaching a curse or a spell. Secondly, it is associated with taunting funerary lamentation (Is 14 1ff.), and with *hôy* (Mic 2 4 Hab 2 6) in contexts that lead Johnson to observe: "Each of these has a dirge-like quality, and each anticipates some form of retribution which will make the person or persons concerned an object-lesson in the abuse of power" (166). To Johnson's references we add Ez 24 3ff., a section of great significance for our association of *hôy* (here *'ôy*, but probably — by way of an exceptional usage — synonymous in meaning with *hôy*; see above, 25) with revenge. See also below, 65, n. 86.

announcement of evil (רעה, verse 3) along the lines of a reversal of the situation indicated in verses 1-2[83].

The *hôy* of Mic 2, then, is directed again at that category of haughty covenant breakers who overrule Israel's sacred covenant traditions in their assumed autonomy. Their punishment will again have the quality of reversal, and it will come from the Lord (verse 3) on "that day" (verse 4), a day of lamentation. The relation of the opening *hôy* to the funerary lamentation is that of anticipation (cf. 1 8. 12!) of the occasion for mourning[84].

While the precise literary relationship of 2 1-5 to chapter 1 is viewed variously, both sections are undisputedly authentic. Even if they should not form a literary unity as they stand, the historical context of this prophet's message demands that we see in the approaching disaster of 1 10ff. that day of punishment and mourning from the Lord against Jerusalem (verse 12) which is also announced in 2 3-5, a punishment which evokes anticipatory mourning (1 8. 16) because it will bring in death and lamentation. This context, and the fact that Micah does not use the terminology of funerary lament anywhere else but in the section preceding the *hôy*-pericope and in that pericope itself, offer at least circumstantial evidence for Micah's consciousness of the derivation of *hôy* from the realm of funerary lamentation. Again, however, the use of *hôy* has undergone the same specialization in the direction of a sombre threat of retribution observed in Amos and Isaiah already.

VII. Habakkuk 2 6-19

Next to Isaiah, it is the Book of Habakkuk that contains the most significant clustering of *hôy*-words: Hab 2 6. 9. 12. 15. 19. In con-

---

[83] Alt sees here a prophetic judgement against the upper classes of Jerusalem, a word which announces to them a coming re-distribution of the lands amassed by them, along the lines of the ancient sacral land rights, a re-distribution by lot in the קהל of Yahweh (verse 5), from which the greedy covenant breakers would be excluded. This interpretation makes good sense of the passage and seems plausible, although our conclusions with respect to *hôy* would not be affected by an understanding of the pericope as announcing punishment in a more general sense to the rich covenant breakers and their city.

[84] The variation possible within the pattern "Alas now ... for the time when 'alas' will be called for, will come" is illustrated by a comparison of this pericope to Am 5 16-20 and Jer 22 13-19. In summary, Mic 2 1-5: The prophet exclaims "*hôy!*" because the time will come when mocking mourners will sing their lamentation. Am 5 16-20: The time of mourning will come (verses 16-17), so that it is already appropriate to start (verses 18-20). Jer 22 13-19: The prophet exclaims "*hôy!*", because the time will come when mourning will be called for, but when no mourner will take it up.

trast to the woe-chains of Isaiah, both metrical and thematic uniformity links the first four of these into a sequence that is almost
certainly original to their composition. The last woe is generally considered secondary. We turn now to a more detailed analysis of Hab
2 6-17.

The four woe-passages of Hab 2 6b-17 show the following formal
features: (1) The opening *hôy*. (2) A participle introducing a description of the addressee. (3) Expansion of the description, varying in
length. Transition to the second person may begin in this expansion
already, or in the following announcement. (4) Announcement of
retribution in terms of reversion of his crime upon the addressee.
(5) Expansion of the description of the retribution, varying in length.
The chain of several *hôy*-stanzas is in itself a characteristic. We note
the absence of any messenger-formulae and their subsequent prophetic "Therefore." As the nations are the speakers in the present
context (2 5b-6a) this does not surprise, but in view of the disputed
nature of that introduction[85], as well as the haphazard distribution
of such formulae in the *hôy*-passages elsewhere, we may interpret
their absence here as further evidence of the tension of the dynamics
of *hôy* with those of the prophetic *Gerichtsrede*.

The prose introduction of verse 2 6a calls the following woes מָשָׁל,
מְלִיצָה and חִידָה. The textual witnesses vary in the grammatical
relationship between the last two, which are set off from מָשָׁל by the
verb. The line suggests either an overlaid bi-colon balancing מָשָׁל with
one or more related terms, or a secondary attachment of these to מָשָׁל.
The same enumeration occurs in Prov 1 6 where, though late, it seems
more appropriate as to form, content and meter. As it contains the
only other instance of מְלִיצָה, an influence from there is most likely.
מָשָׁל, on the other hand, is a good prophetic term, with a range of
meaning capable of spanning the whole continuum from taunting
lamentation to bitter invective[86]. Its application to *hôy*-words not

---

[85] Attempts have been made to reconstruct a woe from Hab 2 5-6a; cf. BHmg, and Elliger, Das Buch der zwölf Kleinen Propheten, II 1967⁶, 41. The tendency to suspect
behind the article in the vicinity of a *hôy*-series an original *hôy* must be resisted, however, unless other evidence supports such an assumption. For a review of textual problems see W. H. Brownlee, The Placarded Revelation of Habakkuk, JBL 82 (1963),
319—325. Brownlee also makes a good case for a reconstructed text without *hôy*.
[86] See above, 63, n. 82, and the article by A. R. Johnson cited there. We add these
observations: Out of some 39 occurrences of מָשָׁל, 12 stand in prophetic books; 8 of
them in Ezekiel. To take up (נשא) a מָשָׁל is an expression used in a *hôy*-passage in
Mic 2 4, in parallelism with "wailing and bitter lamentation" (נהה נהי). Especially
interesting is its use in introducing Balaam's "blessings" (inverted curses!) and curses
(Num 23 7. 18 24 3. 15. 20. 21. 23), including 24 23: "Alas (*ôy*), who shall live . . ."
In Dt 28 37 מָשָׁל follows the covenant curses, and in Jer 24 9 it stands in parallelism,

only agrees well with the death-mourning-vengeance continuum which has been established as the range of *hôy*, but may be taken as further evidence for that range.

The theme of vengeance in kind embraces every one of the four woes of Hab 2 6b-17. Elliger's attempt to see an order of progression, though cautious, is not convincing, although he correctly states that all of them contribute to one comprehensive image (*Gesamtbild*)[87]. While the oppressor is depicted as an individual, verses 8 and 13 indicate that an oppressor of nations is meant[88]. His precise historical identification hinges on one's understanding of 1 6 and the Book of Habakkuk as such. It is not at all unsuitable to think of the Babylonians, at least in the present context[89]. Humbert's detailed analysis of the vocabulary indicates at least the essential contemporaneity of our passage with the foregoing segment of Habakkuk and sets the time as approximately the end of the seventh century B. C.[90]. While no names appear, except "Lebanon," historical situations seem to be implied[91], although the language is full of imagery and must not be pressed for too precise detail.

The first woe, verse 6b-8, offers grave textual difficulties. We reconstruct: הוי־מרבה־לו֯ ¹ ... ² מכביד על־עבטיט "Woe to him who heaps up for himself . . ., who makes heavy the 'yoke' of debt."[92]

---

among other terms, to "curse" (קללה). In Ez 24 3 it introduces a blood-vengeance passage containing two instances of *'ôy*, and in Is 14 4 an (ironical) lamentation for the dead king of Babylon.

[87] K. Elliger, Das Buch der zwölf Kleinen Propheten II, 48.

[88] P. Humbert (Problèmes du Livre d'Habacuc 293 et passim) thinks of Jehoiakim, but Horst (Die Zwölf Kleinen Propheten 168) rightly objects that there is too little evidence to think of an exploitation of other peoples by Jehoiakim as the historical occasion. Humbert (chapter IV) reviews the various positions taken on this question.

[89] Brownlee (The Placarded Revelation 321-325) revocalizes the relative pronoun *'šr* (2 5) to read *'Aššûr* (Assyria), so that the woes of chapter 2 would be spoken by the nations, being liberated by Babylon, against Assyria in her death pangs. He sees here a parallel to the Book of Nahum. This interpretation is appealing, though the "then-now" contrast in the individual woes demands a point in time prior to the final destruction of Assyria.

[90] Humbert, Problèmes du Livre d'Habacuc, chapter III.

[91] Perhaps this is the reason for the ,,riddle(s)" in 2 6a ?

[92] Verse 6 b offers difficulties that are not remedied satisfactorily by excising — as most commentators do — the phrase עד מתי, though that is undoubtedly necessary; it is a cliché introduced by someone who felt himself to share the oppression, or it may reflect later liturgical use of the book. καιγε omits it. 1 Qp Hab tries to smooth the bi-colon by making עד מתי the opening of a new sentence, which required the transformation of the participle מכביד into a finite form יכביד. If we postulate מרבה לו (LXX πληθύνων ἑαυτῷ) as original, it would require an object, as the parallel colon also suggests. In the second colon a rare word, עבטיט, now known to mean "weight

עבטיט means debt for pledges. In our reconstruction we take it to mean that the yoke of debt (for pledges) is heavy upon the oppressed. If עליו were read, it could be understood reflexively: "he loads upon himself debt (for pledges)", i. e. he himself, through exacting booty, or that which does not belong to him, becomes the debtor to those whose property he has taken. The understanding of "your creditors" hinges on the foregoing. The translation as given emphasizes the contrast "you are a harsh creditor . . . harsh creditors will suddenly arise for you". The alternate understanding implies: "You have indebted yourself . . . your creditors will make you pay." In either case the couplet shows that reversal of imagery which we found to characterize many hôy-words. "Suddenly" (verse 7) may be taken together with "to set his nest on high to escape from the grasp of evil" (verse 9b), and perhaps "The cup . . . will come round to you" (verse 16b) and seen in the vengeance context: The one who has incurred blood guilt has reached safety, in his opinion, but the avenger will nevertheless overtake him.

The next woe, verses 9-10, directs itself against an oppressor who deems himself to have "gotten away to his nest"[93] and feels secure there. "A shameful thing" (verse 10) is the evaluation from the standpoint of the speaker, not of the oppressor. Verse 10b is enigmatic and lends itself to various interpretations. Destruction is perhaps implied, as well as some form of antiphonal chant or cry among the ruins.

---

of pledges, heavy debts" (BDB: Akk. ubbuṭu' — be pledged; Aram. עבט — to pledge), sparked another sequence of misunderstandings. LXX has τὸν κλοιὸν αὐτοῦ στιβαρῶς, probably for עליו עבטיט, construing the elements עָב "thicket" (Jer 4 29) or עֳבִי "thickness" (several instances) and טיט "mud" adverbially. If the suffix עליו was in the Vorlage (cf. עלו in 1Q), it may show the older defective orthography for עליו, or it may have been עלו, in which case it could not have stood in construct to עבטיט, thus pointing to a loss of understanding of עבטיט in the Vorlage already. The strangely defective עבט in 1Q, though not its only defective spelling, may show that this word was not understood and therefore not subjected to standardization according to full orthography. There is no clear evidence to decide in favour of the originality of על "yoke" (with a later addition of the suffix) or עליו "upon/against him". Codex Venetus omits the suffix.

[93] The image of the nest on high is significant. קן occurs 12 times. Six times a bird's nest is either meant literally, or it is a part of a simile or image within which it is unterstood literally and expresses security. Of the remainder, besides Hab 2 9, five passages (Is 10 14 16 2 Jer 49 16 Obad 4 Num 24 21) are excellent examples of the themes of escape from revenge, feeling of security, yet ultimate execution of vengeance. All are directed against nations (Assyria, Moab, Edom, Edom, the Kenites, respectively). Is 10 14 stands in a hôy-passage and Num 24 21 in a curse. Jer 49 16 and Obad 4 are associated with imagery akin to Hab 2 15f. These observations confirm the understanding of the woes of Hab 2 as directed against a foreign nation, as well as the vengeance-dimension discovered earlier as a possibility for hôy.

Possibly the unjustly acquired building materials enter into a chant and response of vengeance (*Wechselgesang von Anklage und Fluch*)[94]. Elliger thinks of the exchange of words in court involving accuser and witnesses who speak for the oppressed people who have been silenced[95]. It is also possible that vengeance, in form of destruction of the wrongfully acquired house, is seen in anticipation as having been accomplished already, and no mourners are left but the personified ruins (cf. Lam 2 8, and, with reference to praise, Luke 19 40)[96].

The theme of the third woe, verses 12-13. 17[97], is exploitation. According to generally held interpretation, the "fire" (verse 13) is, perhaps, the fire of destruction brought over the nations by the oppressor as soon as they have accomplished anything. It may, however, be the fire that will destroy the works built up by forced labour. Jer 51 58 supports the latter alternative. We may, then, have here a brief allusion to the Lord's Holy War of vengeance against the oppressor who, with the help of the oppressed peoples, has built up his realm.

Verse 17 offers grave difficulties. The reference to חמס לבנון and שד בהמות is generally taken to imply that the oppressor has ruthlessly cut down trees on the Lebanon and has cruelly driven the beasts of burden employed to transport the timber[98]. If this were correct, the reversal of the crime upon the criminal in such a way that the crime itself acts as the agent of punishment would represent vengeance in its most direct form. It would be more natural to expect an agent of punishment, however, as in the similar passages Jer 46 8 and Obad

---

[94] Horst, Die Zwölf Kleinen Propheten, 181f.

[95] Das Buch der zwölf Kleinen Propheten 46.

[96] The personification of objects into mourners of the deceased with whom they have been associated is a widespread mourning phenomenon; cf. Jahnow 102f.

[97] The transposition of verse 17 to conclude the pericope 12-13 is generally accepted. Verse 13a is a gloss. Verse 14 is a prose insertion that may have entered here instead of the expected announcement of vengeance, after verse 17 had become displaced. For יְחִיתַן (verse 17a) read יְחָתְּךָ, as has long been suggested on the basis of LXX and Syriac. The יחתת of 1Q p Hab may support this if, as Elliger thinks (Studien zum Habakuk-Kommentar, 1953, 57), a כ has been omitted and the ה represents the final letter of the suffix in plene spelling: יחתת[כ]ה.

[98] The theme of the cutting down of the trees of Lebanon by a ruthless invader occurs in Is 14 8, in the ironical lament for the dead kind of Babylon, and in II Kings 19 23 (Is 37 24) where Sennacherib is the guilty party. Then it is also an image for the Lord's punishment (Ez 17 21-22, metaphorically; Zech 11 1-3), sometimes through an agent (Is 10 34 Jer 22 6f.). We have here further evidence that a foreign nation is addressed in our Habakkuk-passage. The animals inhabiting Lebanon are called חיה (II Kings 14 9 Is 40 16 Ez 31 6. 13). The suggestion that the בהמות (verse 17) are the animals exploited and maltreated in hauling logs from Lebanon is, therefore, preferable to the assumption that the wildlife cf Lebanon is meant. But see below, and n. 100.

10[99]. The difficulties of historical interpretation would be avoided, however, if we see here a reference to the violence done to Lebanon and to the wild ox of the wilderness in the mythical past[100].

That vengeance is the basic motif here is certain. The reference to the "blood (pl.) of men" (verse 17b) strengthens this conclusion[101]. The blood may refer to the town built with "blood" (pl.; verse 12). The "violence of the land" is the violence of the oppressor committed in the land, although a passage like Gen 6 13 raises the question whether the territory itself might not have been seen as contaminated by the acts performed in it. This "violence" evoked the avenging "violence of Lebanon", by the way of "reversal of imagery". The reference to "blood" (pl.) will have determined the choice of the verb כסה, associated with blood in the context of blood vengeance (cf. Ez 24 7f. Gen 37 26 Is 26 21 Job 16 18).

The fourth woe, verses 15-16[102], employs drinking imagery to announce a coming reversal of fate: He who has made others drunk will himself be made drunk. This imagery is frequent in expressions of divine retribution against the nations[103]. The content of the cup is national calamity, and Yahweh is the avenger (verse 16b).

---

[99] Note the Day of Yahweh-context, especially in Jer 46 8. The oppressor of the Habakkuk-pericope under discussion fulfills a parallel role to that of Egypt in this passage.

[100] Cf. Von Soden, Das Gilgamesch-Epos, Fünfte Tafel. Prof. F. M. Cross, Jr., has drawn my attention to the possibility that we might have here a reference to the deified giant Lebanon and to the ox of the wilderness.

[101] The "blood (pl.) of men" (verse 17b) may refer to the town built with blood (verse 12). A cursory survey of דם indicates a frequent, though not exclusive, association of the plural with blood-guilt (II Sam 3 28 16 8 I Kings 2 5. 31 II Kings 9 7. 26 Is 4 4 Hos 1 4). The form occurs only in one other place, II Sam 3 28, where David declares himself and his kingdom guiltless of the blood (מדמי) of Abner. This strengthens the already evident vengeance-character of our passage.

[102] Verse 15c is a gloss. The reading הרעל for הערל (verse 16a), long held on the basis of LXX, is now substantiated by 1Qp Hab.

[103] The "cup" rarely holds a positive fate (Ps 16 5 23 5 116 13), but is a frequent symbol for God's wrath, both through an agent (Babylon, implied or expressed: Is 51 17-23 Jer 51 7-8 Ez 23 32) and directly (Ps 11 6 75 9 Lam 4 21 Jer 25 15-29 49 12f.). The cup of wrath returns to those who have given it to others: Is 51 22f. (to Babylon) Lam 4 21 (to Edom) Jer 49 12f. (to Edom). Drinking imagery strikingly similar to our passage appears in the last-mentioned instance, as well as in Jer 25 15-29 and, without the cup, in Obad 16. In short, the imagery of Hab 2 15-16 belongs to the realm of speech associated with retribution and punishment directed against nations. This fact is recognized in the introduction Hab 2 5b-6a, whether original or an addition. Of course, there are admonitions against drunkenness in wisdom literature, but the passages cited show that it is quite unwarranted to take the imagery of Hab 2 15-16 as evidence for any wisdom associations of *hôy*.

The fifth woe, verses 19-18[104], directed against idol worshippers, is clearly recognizable as a later generalization, after the specific content of verses 6b-17 had become blurred into a general indictment against impiety.

In contrast to the forcefully advanced vengeance-motif, the woes of Hab 2 do not evidence any direct awareness of the background of *hôy* in funerary lamentation. The tone is bitter and threatening throughout. The scene is international in extent, and the avenger is Yahweh. With the exception, perhaps, of "fire" (verse 13), the technical terminology of Holy War or of the Day of the Lord is absent, but the general picture is consonant with that established as the context for *hôy* in the eighth-century prophets.

VIII. The Remaining Woes

The remainder of the *hôy*-passages is scattered throughout various prophetic writings. The relationship of the *hôy* in Nah 3 1 to the preceding and the following material is not clear in detail, yet the main lines are evident: Verses 2 6-10 (Heb. 7-11) introduce us to a scene of desolation, followed in verses 11-12 (Heb. 12-13) by questions designed to contrast the present with Nineveh's secure and untouchable power in the past. Whether this "once-now" contrast is evidence of a conscious (mocking) use of the style of funerary lament remains a matter of opinion. The desolation — still in the future — will be the result of the Lord's vengeance described in terms that take up the descriptive terminology (כפירים, טרף; verse 13; Heb. 14)[105] used earlier.

That the *hôy* of 3 1 introduces a new section is generally assumed, but the homogeneity of the Nahum-material is such that a conscious association with the foregoing cannot be denied[106]. The *hôy* definitely stands in a context of death and revenge, followed by further death imagery (3 3) and, perhaps, a further reflection of the style of funerary

---

[104] This order is generally accepted.

[105] A "*Hôy* Nineveh" to open 2 13 (Heb 2 14), as BHmg suggests, would fit perfectly into the contrast of the guilt of the past with the vengeance held out for the future, so typical of vengeance-expressions, but textually it is a pure guess (see above, 65, n. 85), and to adduce it to support our thesis would be circular reasoning.

[106] We cannot discuss the composition of the Book of Nahum in detail here. Whether we are dealing with essentially one long poem, 1 11 — 3 19, as C. Taylor argues (The Interpreter's Bible VI 953—956), or oracles of Nahum, as Horst believes (Die Zwölf Kleinen Propheten 153f.), hardly affects our assumption that it is proper to adduce the context, consisting, by and large, of the whole book, to the elucidation of the *hôy*-cry of 3 1.

lament (verse 7). That the military attack against Nineveh is understood here as the earthly manifestation of the march of the Divine Warrior is proferred in 1 2-6[107].

The two *hôy*-words of Zephaniah (2 5 3 1), though directed at the "nation of the Cherethites" and Jerusalem, respectively, share their setting within the prophet's grand proclamation of the Day of the Lord and the concomitant devastation and wailing of all nations. A more immediate formal context is lacking for the brief woe against the Cretans/Philistines. The woe of 3 1 represents the transition from the series of foreign nations oracles to prophecies concerning Jerusalem but, as Elliger notices correctly[108], a transition that links the two series more than it divides. Jerusalem is not contrasted with the foreign nations, but is drawn, perhaps editorially, into their list and threatened with the same prospect, namely the Day of the Lord.

It can hardly be accidental that the *hôy* follows upon the mocking funerary lamentation against Nineveh (2 15), a city with which Jerusalem shares also the accusation of apparently secure independence. A reminiscence of the funerary background of *hôy* may well be reflected in this succession of *hôy* upon the mocking lament. The basic feature shared by the two passages (2 15 3 1ff.) is the "then-now" theme of funerary lamentation, extended into the "now-future" contrast of vengeance.

The nine genuine and two (48 1 50 27) disputed Jeremianic *hôy*-words include five instances of the standard mourning formula: 22 18 (4×) 34 5. The full range of *hôy* is played in 22 13-19. That the interplay of *hôy* in verse 13 and, on the basis of LXX in verse 18[109],

---

[107] This cosmic dimension of the context of *hôy* would be less explicit if Taylor (The Interpreter's Bible VI 954) were right in ascribing the acrostic (?) poem, 1 2-10, to an editor. Even then, one could argue that the editor properly supplied the expected context for the prophetic understanding of the divine involvement in the fall of nations.

[108] Das Buch der zwölk Kleinen Propheten 75.

[109] LXX omits Ώ (= הוי), probably due to haplography; cf. BHmg.

The phrase Οὐαὶ ἐπὶ τὸν ἄνδρα τοῦτον (= האיש הזה־(?)הוי על) has perhaps fallen out due to homoioteloiton. Its absence in the Lucianic and Hexaplaric manuscripts must be due to the influence of MT; the LXX of Jeremiah is a short text, not given to expansion.

The fourfold *hôy* of verse 18 is textually somewhat unstable. The LXX manuscripts have two links in the chain, corrections towards the MT excepted. The somewhat difficult form הדה has led M. J. Dahood (CBQ 23, 1961, 462—464; cited in J. Bright, Jeremiah, 1965, 142) to suggest a change to *hōrāh*, so as to obtain the enumeration "Ah, brother! Ah, sister! Ah, father ['âdôn]! Ah, mother!", all referring to the king "who was (so in Phoenician texts) supposed to be father, mother, sister and brother to his people." The case cannot be decided, but the fourfold enumeration,

with traditional funerary cry "*hôy* my brother . . .", etc., (verse 18) is
not only conscious but represents the dominating dynamic of this
pericope, is clear from the passage itself, but receives added confirma-
tion from a comparison with 22 10. There Jehoiakim's father Josiah,
the contrasting model held up before Jehoiakim in verses 15-16, is
juxtaposed to the other son, Jehoahaz, in the same sequence: "Weep
not for [Josiah] . . . but weep bitterly for [Jehoahaz]", for the former
does not need it, while the latter is as good as dead in a foreign land.
The contrast can, of course, refer only to the manner of death: burial
by respectful posterity that performs the due rituals faithfully[110], as
compared to death and burial away from land and kindred. Just as
the latter calls for weeping (בכה) now, because there will conceivably
be no weeping later, at the time of actual death, so Jehoiakim's situation calls for a *hôy* now (verses 13. 18a LXX), because there will be
no *hôy* later (verse 18).

  While firmly rooted in the funerary context, however, the woe-
pericope verses 13-17, considered independently of verses 18-19, shows
all the characteristics of theme and form discovered for prophetic
hôy-words in our study so far. Jehoiakim is accused of self-centred
oriental despotism resulting in flagrant transgression of covenant
obligations — thus invoking the contrasting image of his father! —
to the point of blood guilt (verse 17). As to formal features, the *hôy*
is followed by a participle expanded by finite verbs in the third person, but probably intended again as an expanded address, as is
indicated by the characteristic turn to second-person speech as soon
as the predication is completed. As often in *hôy*-pericopes, the second-
person address takes the form of a rhetorical question[111]. In brief,
22 13-17, without verses 18-19, represents a *typical* prophetic *hôy*-word.

  This suggests one of two conclusions: It may be that the *hôy* of
other prophetic contexts where no funerary associations are evident
is to be read with the assumption that the ties to funerary lamentation

---

  whether original or secondarily expanded from a twofold repetition (LXX), is in
  keeping with mourning rites.

    אחי, "my brother", with MT, is preferable over LXX's standardized "brother;"
  we have here the firmly coined mourning formula of a sister, for it was the sister who
  was the principal mourner for her brother (Jahnow 63 ff.). D. N. Freedman (in a pri-
  vate communication made available to the writer by Prof. G. E. Wright) points out
  that the suffixes of "brother" and "lord" are good examples of Dahood's and G. R.
  Driver's "double duty suffix": "*Hôy*, my brother! *Hôy* [my] sister! *Hôy*, [his]
  lordship! *Hôy*, his majesty!"

[110] See Jer 34 5 for the *hôy*-cry as a part of proper burial for a king. The strange reading
  of several LXX[B] manuscripts καὶ ἕως ᾅδου is, no doubt, explained correctly in
  BHmg as an inner-Greek corruption: ω(ει)αδων.

[111] See above, 47, n. 18.

were sufficiently clear to be invoked by the *hôy* itself. It is also possible, however, that *hôy* had taken on a specialized function in prophecy by Jeremiah's time, a function which, though not necessarily fully at the expense of its funerary background, had developed away from its central function there, namely the expression of mourning and grief, and had come to express anger and vengeance, a content that, as we have shown, is still within the field of dynamics of the funerary cry, though not at its center. Jeremiah, then, in full awareness of this specialization of *hôy* and using it in that specialized manner in verses 13-17, has heightened its effectiveness by juxtaposing it in verse 18 to the funerary cry in its central mourning significance.

Jer 23 1-8 concludes the series of oracles against the royal house, introduced in 21 11. The opening *hôy* may form a bridge, by catchword-connection, to 22 13-18. It summarizes the attitude of Jeremiah to the royal house of his time. The pericope clearly consists of at least three segments: verses 1-4. 5-6 and 7-8. The unity even of 1-4 is not uncontested[112], so that a minimal claim leads to a core oracle made up of verses 1-2. In this *Gerichtsrede in nuce*, however, we note the characteristic marks of *hôy* as studied so far. Punishment consists of reversal of fate, expressed most clearly through the double sense in which פקד is used. As in so many other woes, the Lord's vengeance is directed against the upper echelon, in contrast to the poor and oppressed people (עמי) whose *gō'ēl* is the Lord. Whether the speaker of the woe proper (verse 1) is the prophet or the Lord cannot be decided in the present distended prose form of the oracle[113]. External evidence of a mourning context consists only of the passage's loose relationship to 22 13-18.

The *hôy* of Jer 30 7 is textually uncertain, being absent from the Greek manuscript families with the exception of the Hexaplaric. A transposition from הוי to היו (ἐγενήθη) is easy to assume, but can also be regarded as a smoothing out, as over against the *lectio difficilior* of MT. Metrically the longer היו would be better. As to context, *hôy* would be most appropriate as an introduction marking the Day of the Lord, but for that same reason it might have been attracted to replace a היו. The case remains unresolved.

---

[112] Rudolph (Jeremia 145) treats verse 3 as a later addition, because it assumes the Captivity as a fact, but he allows for the genuineness of verse 4. Bright (Jeremiah 145f.) considers verses 1-4 as basically Jeremianic, though worked over later. For our purposes, verses 1-2 are the verses of interest, irrespective of possible further extent of the unit.

[113] The concluding נאם יהוה is best omitted, with the LXX[B] family and other Greek manuscripts. The pronominal suffix of מרעית could equally fittingly be in the first person singular (MT) or third person plural (LXX).

LXX also disposes of another difficult *hôy* in Jer 47 6, this time by resorting to a reinterpretation possible only by translating the specific Hebrew תתגודדי by a general κόψεις upon which the "sword of the Lord" follows as a vocative. While it might be possible, metaphorically, to say "How long will you smite (κόψεις), sword of the Lord?", one could hardly say "How long will you gash yourself [in mourning], sword of the Lord?", the translation that the Hebrew certainly demands for the Hithpo. of גדד, especially in parallelism to קרח (cf. Jer 16 6 41 5 Dt 14 1)[114]. We have here a *hôy* plus address, a marker of lamentation defined as to its direction precisely by that address, in the context of the lamentation brought on by the Lord's Day against the nations.

The woe of Jer 48 1 is part of a series of Moab-oracles. According to Rudolph[115], whose position is winning wide acceptance, chapter 48 consists of a core of Jeremianic words, supplemented freely from earlier oracles, notably Is 15—16 in the case of 48 29-39, and Num 21 27-30 in the case of 48 45-46[116]. The more immediate unit which *hôy* opens consists of verses 1-10[117]. The Holy War motifs of this unit are unmistakable[118]. Weeping is mentioned in verse 5, taken from Is 15 5, where

---

[114] The LXX use of κόπτω is clever, as it means "to smite" as well as "to mourn", probably because of the practice of mourners to smite their breasts. Its derivative noun κοπετός means "funerary lamentation". Nevertheless, the present translation is a *tour de force*. One wonders, further, whether the helplessness of LXX with reference to a *hôy* supposedly considered atypical — but not so in our understanding of it! — may not be reflected also in 30 7.

[115] Rudolph, Jeremia, 277—284. Cf. also Bright, Jeremiah, 322f.; R. Bach, Die Aufforderungen zur Flucht und zum Kampf im alttestamentlichen Prophetenspruch, 1962, 25, notes 1 and 2.

[116] Verses 45-47 are lacking in LXX; they are additions to the chapter by a later hand; in the case of verses 45f. from Num 21 27-30. The editor seems to have intended a closing which rounds off the chapter by a return to the opening. See above, 25ff.

[117] With Rudolph (Jeremia 278, including n. 1) against Kuschke (Jeremia 48 1-8. Zugleich ein Beitrag zur historischen Topographie Moabs, in: Verbannung und Heimkehr, ed. by A. Kuschke, 1961, 181—196), who argues for verses 1-8 as a unit. In contrast to Rudolph, we understand verse 10 as a part of the Holy War context, rather than a gloss. Against Rudolph's statement that it would hardly be necessary to spur Nebuchadnezzar to wield his sword diligently, one can say that we have here a curse against slackness in the pursuit of Holy War (Judg 5 23; cf. also I Kings 20 42 I Sam 15 23b Judg 21 5 I Sam 11 7). Non-participation or slack participation in Holy War seems to be a neglected aspect in the study of that institution.

[118] The "summons to flee," verses 6-8, has been shown by R. Bach (Die Aufforderungen zur Flucht und zum Kampf 15ff.) to belong to a prophetic genre rooted in Holy War ideology. The admittedly loose association with the War Song of the Ammonites (verses 45f.), based on Num 21 27-30 (cf. Miller, Holy War and Cosmic War in Early Israel) and the curse of verse 10 (see above, n. 117) contribute further to the Holy War motif in the passage under discussion.

the context of funerary lament is pronounced. The further chapter is full of wailing and mourning terminology. This may suggest conscious employment of *hôy* in awareness of its background in funerary lament, yet the structure of the chapter is too loose to allow certainty in this respect. At best we can say that *hôy*, introduced as divine speech, opens a long oracle in which Holy War motifs and mourning language are amply represented.

The long oracle against Babylon, Jer 50 1—51 58, is no less complex, nor is its authenticity less contested[119]. Rudolph's detailed argumentation against Jeremianic authorship[120] holds the field, by and large, in spite of Eissfeldt's attempt to refute it[121]. There is general agreement however, that the prophecy stands close to Jeremiah in time, for not only is the end of Babylon portrayed as a future event, but it is pictured in catastrophic terms that approximate in no way the almost peaceful take-over by Cyrus[122].

The *hôy* (verse 27) stands in the immediate context of verses 21-28[123], a call of Yahweh to his agent of destruction to wage Holy War against Babylon. Rudolph's succinct characterization deserves to be cited:

Jahwe fordert sein Strafwerkzeug auf, den Kampf gegen Babel in der schärfsten Form des „Bannes", d. h. (Jdc 6 21. 24 1 S 15 3) der völligen Vernichtung der Menschen, Tiere und Sachen zu führen (vgl. 26f.). Und wie er befiehlt, so geschiehts: schon ist der Krieg im Lande, schon ist der Zusammenbruch da (22, vgl. 4 6 6 1), und schon kann man das höhnische[124] Klagelied über Babel anstimmen (23), das dem Umschwung der Dinge Ausdruck gibt . . . An diese seine Werkzeuge [die Jahwe zur Verfügung stehenden Völker] ergeht in 26f. erneut sein Aufruf, der v. 21 wieder aufnimmt: zur Vollstreckung des Bannes sollen alle Speicher geöffnet und ihr Inhalt auf offenem Markt ausgeschüttet und restlos verbrannt werden, wie es das Gesetz vorschreibt (Dt 13 17) . . . so nimmt der Gott Israels Rache an einem Volk, das das von ihm erwählte Volk angriff.[125]

---

[119] For a survey of various positions, see O. Eissfeldt, Jeremias Drohorakel gegen Babel, in: Verbannung und Heimkehr, 31—37.

[120] Rudolph, Jeremia, 297—299.

[121] Eissfeldt, Jeremias Drohorakel, op. cit., especially 34f.

[122] Bright, Jeremiah, 360.

[123] Verse 28 not only belongs to the foregoing, in spite of metrical difficulties (cf. RSV), but is the motive and occasion (*Zielpunkt*) of this section, as Rudolph (Jeremia 303) correctly observes; it is the escape of Israel from Babylon which is at issue. For formal analysis of a "summons to flee," as well as its place and function within Holy War, see R. Bach, Die Aufforderungen zur Flucht und zum Kampf. The verse under consideration is, strictly speaking, no such summons, but a description of its effect. The form proper is present in 50 8-10 51 6 51 46 (Bach 17ff.).

[124] See below, n. 126.

[125] Rudolph, Jeremia, 303.

We observe here the association of *hôy* with funerary lamentation (verses 23. 27; cf. 51 8. 41ff.), and that within the context of vengeance in kind — a theme pervading the whole oracle most persistently (50 15. 28. 29 51 6ff. 11. 24. 35f. 49. 56) — wrought through the Lord's Holy War to bring in the "day" (כִּי־בָא יוֹם עֵת פְּקֻדְתָם, 50 27b; cf. 50 31 51 2. 47. 52). The precise place of *hôy* on the emotional continuum between sorrowful lamentation and threatening invective cannot be determined even here, however[126]. One wonders, both here and else-where, whether it was not this very breadth of emotional range which led to the employment of *hôy* in a context such as this.

Of the three *hôy*-occurrences of Ezekiel (13 3. 18 and 34 2), 34 2 can certainly not be considered apart from Jer 23, a chapter intro-duced by *hôy* which treats the theme of false shepherds, and 13 3. 18 also seem to reflect that chapter, with its woe against unreliable leaders. The influence may not have extended far beyond a general stimulus; as to their details the Ezekiel-passages are rather indepen-dent in form and content. Nevertheless, the employment of *hôy* can hardly be regarded to be an altogether deliberate choice of the prophet, but must be seen as due to external suggestion.

For chapter 13, Zimmerli has demonstrated in a careful form-critical analysis a cohesive unit consisting of two oracles against prophets and prophetesses respectively, oracles introduced by the *hôy*-words of verse 3 and verse 18, and constructed in conscious par-allelism[127]. In a general way these oracles share with the earlier woes their thrust against the self-willed independence from the Lord on the part of certain leading groups. While the pericopes in question unfold according to the dictates of Ezekiel's style and do not, by and large, show the content discovered as characteristic for the setting of *hôy*, we do note the rhetorical questions (verses 7 and 18) and, much more important, the explicit association of *hôy* with the Day of the Lord (verse 5; also verses 13f.)[128].

---

[126] Rudolph, in the quotation just cited, assumes that the lament of verse 23 is taunting ("das höhnische Klagelied"). He follows here the general tendency of commentators to assume that a prophetic lament over one accused or threatened, whether Israelite or foreigner, cannot be meant to convey a mood other than a taunting one ("Spott; spöttisch"). This appears to assume a simplistic psychology. We hold that it is quite possible to cry out in serious and emphathetic awe at the sight or prospect of the destruction of an enemy through the numenous forces at work in a divinely led history.

In the present case, however, the similarity of the *hôy*-verse to verse 31, where threat, rather than mourning, is obvious, makes it probable that the *hôy* was meant to carry a threat, even though that does not exclude all mourning content.

[127] W. Zimmerli, Ezechiel, 1957—, 285ff.

[128] Zimmerli (ibid. 294) correctly identifies the phenomena of these verses with the Day of the Lord.

Ezekiel 34, where the dependence on Jeremiah is patent[129], offers similar conclusions: A rhetorical question follows upon *hôy* (verse 2). A reference to the Day of the Lord — though less explicit than in chapter 13 — can be seen in verse 12. As in chapter 13, the punishment is expressed in the distended prose style of Ezekiel, without any evidence of specific reversal of fate. In both chapters *hôy* has become a part of divine speech[130]. Direct evidence of consciousness of the background of *hôy* in funerary lament is lacking.

As suggested earlier, the two *'ôy*-words of Ez 24 1-14 bear the marks of prophetic woes usually rendered by *hôy*[131]. Zimmerli has given a thorough form-critical analysis of this passage[132]: After an introduction, verses 1-3a, a משל presents an ordinary cooking procedure, verses 3b-5, a procedure, however, which is revealed as to its foreboding character in the image of God's boiling cauldron, Jerusalem, verses 9-10a. Zimmerli considers verses 6-8 to be the result of a reworking (*Nachinterpretation*) which shaped verses 6-10a into the prophetic invective-threat-sequence by premitting the woe of verses 6-8 as an invective to verses 9-10a. The latter, then, receive further expansion. The reworking is ascribed by Zimmerli to Ezekiel, perhaps, but possibly it belongs to his school.

For our purposes the important observations are the secondary incorporation of verses 6-8 into the present *Gerichtswort*-context. This woe, though deriving its content from the historical situation as seen by Ezekiel (cf. 11 5ff.), has its own inner structure as a word of revenge: The *'ôy* is followed by the naming of the "murderer" (עיר הדמים; cf. Nah 3 1; also Hab 2 12), whose brazen blood guilt has not even been "uncharged" by the expected apotropaic ritual (verse 7)[133]. Thereupon the Lord's revenge, provoked deliberately, is announced by the way of reversal of imagery: "She put it [her blood; i. e. the blood shed by her] on the bare rock (verse 7a) . . . I have set on the bare rock her[134] blood (verse 8)." The repetition of the *'ôy*-formula in

---

[129] With Zimmerli (ibid. 835f.), against W. H. Brownlee, Ezekiel's Poetic Indictment of the Shepherds, HTR 51 (1958), 191—203. Brownlee states: "There is nothing to show a dependence of the genuine Ezekiel upon Jeremiah 23 1-2, the doom portion of Jeremiah's similar oracle. The shepherd motif, which is a common one in ancient literature, proves nothing as to literary dependence" (198). In view of the generally recognized ties between the two prophets, this conclusion, based on drastic literary-critical surgery, can hardly convince.

[130] Cf. Zimmerli, Ezechiel, 286 and 832.

[131] See above, 25, 34.

[132] Zimmerli, Ezechiel, 559—561.

[133] Cf. E. Merz, Die Blutrache bei den Israeliten, 1916, 51.

[134] The reversal of imagery to bring out the vengeance would be complete even if "her blood" were to be read here (verse 8), with RSV and the commentators, as referring

verse 9, textually unstable[135], is probably influenced by its earlier occurrence in verse 6, though the secondary unit, verses 6-10a (10b-14), embodies a vengeance thrust also[136]. We note in passing the two-fold *'ôy* of vengeance in the brief gloss in Ez 16 23[137].

Several Exilic or post-Exilic words remain to be considered. Is 33 1 has already been cited and discussed in another connection[138] as a closely-knit woe of vengeance with perfectly balanced reversal of imagery. Childs takes the "destroyer", though unidentified, to be Assyria, a very plausible suggestion, and sees chapter 33 as a later, prophetic reflection on the events of 701[139]. The ties of this woe to the "prophetic liturgy"[140] in which it now stands are too loose to allow us to draw on that context for its elucidation.

The two *hôy*-words introducing proverbs (Is 45 9. 10) and the *hôy* of Is 55 1 have already been discussed[141].

Hôy occurs three times in Zech 2 10-16 (MT; English 2 6-12), a pericope in two parallel parts (verses 10-13 and 14-16), wedged in between Zechariah's third and fourth vision. Interpreters generally assume that the *hôy* of verses 10 (2×) and 11[142] is a call to attention (*Anruf*) quite different from the typical prophetic *hôy*[143]. That such an *Anruf* is not

---

to "the blood she has shed", as it should certainly be read in verse 7. If one were to see a deliberate play on words in these two verses, understanding דמה (verse 7) as the blood she has shed, and דמה (verse 8) as her own blood which the Lord has determined to shed, the already evident sense would be strengthened. Such a reading would also make excellent sense of נתתי, in the first person, a form bothersome to some commentators (BHmg; Eichrodt, Der Prophet Hesekiel, 1966, 224), but textually well supported and not to be changed to נְתָנָה, as Zimmerli (Ezechiel 557) rightly observes. The reading back into verse 7 of the first person construction (τέταχα . . . ἐκκέχυκα; LXX) cannot be upheld, however; it is the attempt of the Greek translators to make sense of נתתי.

[135] The major LXX witnesses omit it, except the Hexaplaric (with asterisk) and Lucianic families. Vulgate has it, but not L^SW. Its authenticity is at least questionable.

[136] For a helpful interpretation of the metallurgical imagery and its center in the terms חלאה "corrosion" and נתך, here "to smelt down", see J. L. Kelso, Ezekiel's Parable of the Corroded Copper Cauldron, JBL 64 (1945), 391—393.

[137] It is absent from LXX; probably the emotional comment of a later scribe.

[138] See above, 22, 35.   [139] Childs, Isaiah, 112—117.

[140] H. Gunkel, Jes 33, eine prophetische Liturgie, ZAW 42 (1924), 177ff.

[141] See above, 56 and 20, including n. 69, respectively; also below, 79, n. 148.

[142] Whether the *hôy* of verse 11, absent from LXX, is a secondary expansion cannot be decided with certainty, but seems likely. The LXX text of verses 10f. seems superior by avoiding the pitfall of mistaking "Zion" for a vocative and making it the (singular) antecedent to the two following verbal forms, a pitfall occasioned in MT by the presence of *hôy* before "Zion". See below, n. 146.

[143] Thus RSV translates "Ho! ho!" and Horst (Die Zwölf Kleinen Propheten 224) "Hei! hei!", in contrast to the usual "woe/wehe."

distinct from the other varieties of *hôy* has already been demonstrated in principle[144]. The words under discussion can be drawn even closer into the circle of the "prophetic *hôy*", however. Basic to an understanding of verses 10-13 is Bach's elucidation of the "summons to flight"[145], a genre to which these verses clearly belong[146]. The relationship of the premitted *hôy*-cries to this genre becomes clear when we give up the attempt to relate them to whatever follows as an *Anruf*. Instead, we have here the *hôy*-"formula" *in nuce*, consisting of the cry alone. It is related to the "summons to flight" in precisely the same manner as the *hôy* of Jer 50 27 to the repeated "summons to flight" of Jer 50 1—51 58[147]: The woe is spoken over the oppressor, whom the Lord's Holy War will crush, while the "summons to flight" is addressed to Israel, for whom the time to escape has come. The fact that this context, spelled out so fully in Jer 50—51, can be assumed, allowing the bare juxtaposition of the two formulae (*"Hôy!"* and "Flee . . .!"), shows that we are dealing with a firmly fixed pattern within which both have their well-defined function[148]. The relationship of *hôy* to the complex of motifs surrounding Holy War and the Day of the Lord receives significant support here.

Our final *hôy*-word, Zech 11 17, allows no certain conclusions concerning its relationship to its context, nor has any consensus emerged with respect to the identity of the worthless shepherd[149]. It seems reasonable to assume that the pronouncement of *hôy* against a shepherd harks back to Jer 23 1 and/or Ez 34 1, even though direct dependence cannot be established beyond doubt. For our purposes it is important to note that *hôy*, at this late stage, is understood as a

---

[144] See above, 18 ff.

[145] R. Bach, Die Aufforderungen zur Flucht und zum Kampf.

[146] Bach discusses this text (ibid. 19). No doubt, he is right in considering verses 10 f. to be prophetic speech, omitting נאם יהוה (2×) as secondary. Verse 10b is an expansion of the genre proper. The conjunction of ונסו (verse 10) should be dropped, with LXX. The singular forms המלטי and יושבת, mistakenly referring to ציון, should be plural forms, הִמָּלְטוּ, and יוֹשְׁבֵי with LXX (thus also Horst, Die Zwölf Kleinen Propheten, 224). ציון is accusativus loci, with LXX and many commentators.

[147] See above, 75 ff.

[148] It is tempting to suggest a similar function for the *hôy* of Is 55 1, a passage which we have interpreted differently in a somewhat *ad hoc* fashion (see above, 20). Could not a "summons to flight" stand behind the promise of salvation contained in Is 55?

[149] Elliger (Das Buch der zwölf Kleinen Propheten 165 f.) considers verse 17 to be a self-contained unit. Horst (Die Zwölf Kleinen Propheten 214. 252 f.) treats 11 4-17 12 7-9 as a unit. R. C. Dentan (The Interpreter's Bible VI 1105) isolates 11 15-17 as an oracle. If Horst were right, the call to the sword of the Lord would call to mind other *hôy*-passages (Jer 47 6 50 35 ff.) in a Holy War context, but we are on too uncertain ground to press any conclusions.

curse, as is shown by its association with typical curse imagery. Of course, one isolated instance, and one that probably employs *hôy* under the influence of earlier associations, is not sufficient to conclude a full-scale development of *hôy*-usage in the direction of the curse. We may well be dealing here with evidence for the loss of awareness of the specific place and function of *hôy* in prophecy.

Chapter 3: The Place and Function of *Hôy* in Prophecy

I. Characterization of *Hôy*

In the previous chapter we have surveyed the *hôy*-pericopes descriptively. It remains to draw certain summarizing conclusions and to ask what it may have been that attracted *hôy* into prophetic usage.

A consideration of *all hôy*-occurrences has led to a devaluation of the significance often attributed to the participle following many a *hôy* and of the characterization of *hôy*-pericopes as directed against social injustice. We found the highlighting of these features to be the result of selective use of evidence. The only formally stable part of the *hôy*-pericopes is the introductory *hôy* itself, followed by an address expressed by a participle, a general noun, or a proper noun. This, it is worth noting, is the basic form of the mourning cry. If the addressee comprises a defined and namable entity, such as a city or a people, he will be represented by a noun, general or proper: "*Hôy*, city!", "*Hôy*, Assur!". If the addressee is a group united only by that characteristic on the basis of which the *hôy* is pronounced, he will be addressed in participial form: "*Hôy*, joining ones house to house!".

While the content of the *hôy*-formula, strictly speaking, can be only that contained in the addressing word or words (such as "sinning people," "wise ones in your own eyes," etc.), the content of the fairly compact and delimitable unit of prophetic speech within which *hôy* stands and which we have called the *hôy*-pericope, though not indicative of any "original" *hôy*-genre, reveals the contextual content within which the prophet considered the use of *hôy* to be fitting. If we can discover any features in it that specify it with greater exactness than the general category of prophetic *Gerichtsrede*, such evidence is valuable in ascertaining the prophetic understanding and use of *hôy*, though not, as has already been emphasized, of discovering a pre-prophetic *hôy*-genre. To do the latter, it would be necessary to demonstrate the possibility of establishing a controllable demarcation line between a stable formula and the general prophetic message surrounding it.

We believe to have discovered the following three features, listed in the order of descending certainty, to be a fairly characteristic though not universal, contextual content of *hôy*: (1) A characterization of the addressee, either from within Israel or representing a foreign nation, as one who acts in self-reliant independence of the sovereignty of Yahweh. This may manifest itself simply in false security, or in group behaviour defiant of covenant obligations towards the poor and needy, or in acts of national-political disloyalty to Yahweh. (2) A "Day of the Lord"-context within which the self-styled sovereignty will be confronted by the greater sovereignty of Yahweh in a terrifying visitation. (3) This confrontation is often expressed in a manner approximating the *Talionsstil*, the style of declaration of revenge, frequently to the point of "reversal of imagery" which, in its most pointed form, takes on the pattern: "You have done X; therefore X will be done to you."

This characterization begs the question of controls. Is not all prophecy directed against haughty covenant-breakers? Is not the Day of the Lord a theme permeating prophecy so widely that almost any prophetic term can be linked to it somehow? Is it not a characteristic of prophecy, and of human nature generally, to "make the punishment fit the crime"? We hasten to re-emphasize that the three features just listed do not represent the *content* of the *hôy*-formula; *hôy* must be characterized as a marker of pain, the direction of which is determined by the addressee named subsequently. These three features represent the prophetic *context* and are, therefore, part and parcel of the main thrust of prophecy. They are, consequently, to be found outside of the *hôy*-pericopes as well. Nevertheless, we contend that the immediate *hôy*-context shows the contrast between the pinnacles of haughty self-reliance and the depths of humiliation on Yahweh's Day, often a contrast that extends into the very vocabulary, with a sharpness and concentration that — though present in other passages — does not characterize prophecy throughout and therefore attracts attention to its frequent presence in the *hôy*-pericope.

It may have been this concentration of intensity of these admittedly widespread prophetic themes that may have led the prophets to explode into the *hôy*-cry at certain points in their message, although it is not to be suggested here that it is possible to rate satisfactorily the *emotional* intensity of prophetic oracles on the basis of literary features and to claim first place for *hôy*-words. The power to express intensely the emotional content of reversal from a desirable to an undesirable state of existence is precisely that capacity which *hôy* brings with it from its place and function within funerary lamentation. There it was the turn from life to death which elicited the *hôy*-cry, and that in a broad range of function with three foci:

(1) He who finds himself in a comparatively desirable state but foresees a turn to the undesirable, (the undesirable which shares in the quality of death, whether it takes the form of sickness, war, catastrophe, or actual death), cries out, "Woe (is me)!" This is the

"'*ôy*-function", expressed generally by the same interjection as funerary lament proper, though separated from *hôy* in the prophetic books by a process of specialization of the latter.

(2) The turn from life to death, i. e. the actual death of someone, elicits the woe-cry ("Woe/alas, brother/sister", etc.) from those close to him, often accompanied by a praise of his life and a bewailing of his present contrasting state.

(3) In the context of murder, where the guilty one has escaped, those close to the victim may break forth into woe-cries ("Woe to him!") expressive of the foreseen and/or planned turn of affairs through which the one who now deems himself safe and secure will be reached by the arm of vengeance, so that the apparent security will turn into death for him.

The following summarizes this range, with its three foci, schematically:

Woe is me!

(1) Acceptable state ___↑___→ calamity, suffering/death (foreseen)

Woe, brother!

(2) Life ___↑___→ death (actual)

Woe unto him!

(3) Escape, security ___↑___→ vengeance/death (foreseen)

It is worth noting that the woe-cry in (2) and (3) is raised by the bystander(s), but even in (1) the situation is not so different; as the cry is uttered in anticipation, the one who foresees a turn for the worse actually becomes a "bystander" for his own future. (Of course, the woe-cry in (1) can also be spoken — and is frequently spoken in the Old Testament — by a bystander, so that its fuller range is "Woe is me/you/him/them!"). This "bystander pronouncement" acquires interest when we consider the function of *'ašrê*; it is, no doubt, one of the factors which eventually attracted the two words to each other.

We observe, then, that the features which our exegetical survey singled out as remarkably characteristic of the immediate context of *hôy* in the prophets work together to heighten the contrast between a state deemed (rightly or wrongly) to be desirable and its grim sequel, a contrast which characterizes the situational context of the woe-cry (in its range established in our first chapter) and elicits it. The inference that we have to see here the point of contact between the funerary background of the woe-cry and the employment of it, as *hôy*, by the prophets seems unavoidable.

II. Sketch of a History of *Hôy* in Prophecy

In the Old Testament the *hôy*-formula has left its non-literary function as a pain-marker, as well as its primary *Sitz im Leben* in the funerary ritual, and has entered upon a literary life within a new historically and literarily definable sphere, prophecy. Our exegetical survey has, we hope, elucidated its place and function within various segments of prophetic literature. It has also furnished some evidence which warrants an attempt to sketch a history of *hôy* within prophecy.

It is impossible to say whether the two *hôy*-occurrences in Amos represent the induction of *hôy* into the service of the prophets, or whether they are merely our earliest extant evidence of an already existing tradition. Their living ties with funerary lament, as well as the fact that the Day of the Lord, a theme with which *hôy* was subsequently to be closely associated, is presented here from an aspect new and surprising to Amos' hearers, may speak for their originality here, or at least for the assumption that we are close to the source of the *hôy*-tradition in prophecy.

Not only in Amos, but also in Isaiah and in the only instance in Micah, that is, in the prophetic use of *hôy* in the eighth century, there is strong evidence for a living awareness of the background of *hôy* in funerary lamentation. In spite of such evidence in Isaiah, however, the majority of his *hôy*-words direct this grief/pain-marker against the God-defying self-reliance of the haughty, making it thereby an expression foreboding evil, without much contextual evidence of mournfulness in many instances. In the earlier *hôy*-words the addressees are, in keeping with the times and the general message, those who disregard their covenant obligations by practicing social injustice. In the prophet's later period he addresses the woes to those who defy the Holy One of Israel by defying his Holy War through political machinations, or against the nations generally who do not acknowledge the Lord's *imperium*.

The first-mentioned group shares the characteristics of those addressed in Am 6 1, which raises the question of dependence, a question that R. Fey has answered in a strongly affirmative way for Amos and Isaiah generally, in a thorough and painstaking study[1]. It is remarkable that Fey, apparently without particular awareness of the fact, or at least without attributing any importance to it, even though that would have strengthened his case, uses as his prime evidence a number of *hôy*-pericopes[2]. Even though Fey has pressed his case to the limits of ingenuity and has been criticized severely by H. W.

---

[1] Fey, Amos und Jesaja, op. cit.
[2] Cf. above 47 ff.

Wolff[3], he has made it appear at least very likely that Isaiah worked with Amos-materials at points, and that the *hôy*-pericope Am 6 1-7 was among these. The relatively similar contextual content of various *hôy*-pericopes in the two prophets would certainly receive elucidation on this basis. The closeness of Micah to Isaiah is common knowledge, and it would not be difficult to assume that Micah's *hôy* shares in the continuity between Amos and Isaiah.

Isaiah has left us the largest single group of extant *hôy*-words, and it is here that we gain our broadest basis for understanding the prophetic use of this formula, as characterized earlier[4]. It is here, also, that a de-emphasizing, if we may cautiously call it this, of the funerary background of *hôy* takes place. This situation poses the question, therefore, what it was that made *hôy* so attractive to Isaiah and what in Isaiah's proclamation may have given his *hôy*-pericopes its stamp[5].

Fichtner[6] characterizes the proclamation of Isaiah as one in which "reversal" (*Umkehrung*) is central, and that in two ways: Israel's sin consists of reversal of loyalty (*Abkehr von Jahwe*). In turn, Yahweh reverses his acts against Israel in such a way as to make the punishment the reversal of the transgressions of the people. Fichtner grants the existence of such reversal elsewhere, but contends:

> Das Ziel der vorliegenden kleinen Studie ist es lediglich, an der Botschaft *eines* Propheten die grundsätzliche Erkenntnis von der „Umkehrung" bis in die Einzelheiten hinein aufzuzeigen. Dafür scheint mir die Botschaft Jesajas besonders gegeben; denn in ihr läßt sich jene Umkehr bis ins Terminologische hinein überraschend klar verfolgen.[7]

He proceeds to portray the reversal of Israel's relationship to Yahweh as one towards haughty rebelliousness:

> Dieser Haltung entspricht einerseits die hochmütige Auflehnung Israels und sein überheblicher Stolz gegenüber Jahwe (2 6ff. 9 9), andererseits die glaubenslose Furcht, die zu eigenen Rüstungen (2 7 7 2) führt (7 1-9 8 12ff.) und der Griff nach der menschlichen Hilfe in der Bündnispolitik (c. 18. 20. 30. 31 u. ö.) und schließlich die Wendung zu anderen Gottheiten (1 29 2 8 17 10ff.). In seiner Hybris setzt sich Israel an Gottes Stelle.[8]

---

[3] Cf. above, 52, n. 34.

[4] The characteristics of the Isaianic use of *hôy* have been summarized above, 61f.

[5] Fichtner's demand (Die „Umkehrung" 459) is well stated: "Ebenso ist die Botschaft dieser [der im Gegensatz zur offiziellen Heilsprophetie stehenden] Propheten nicht in einzelne Gerichtsakte und Heilsbilder aufzulösen, wenn man wirklich erfassen will, worum es ihnen in ihrer Verkündigung geht, sondern man wird dem grundlegenden Motiv nachgehen müssen, das die Gerichts- und Heilsbotschaft beherrscht."

[6] Ibid. 459—466.

[7] Ibid. 459.

[8] Ibid. 461.

The Lord's punishment then constitutes a reversal again: "So wird der Frevel der Hybris durch die Erniedrigung bestraft."[9] Fichtner singles out the place of the woes in this reversal: "Ebenso stellt der Prophet in den Weherufen 5 8ff. dem jeweiligen sündigen Verhalten als Strafe die Umkehrung gegenüber."[10] Finally, he notes that the judgement, which comprises the reversal,

> ist nicht kurzschlüssig als Reaktion auf das Handeln des Menschen aufzufassen, so deutlich es auch darauf bezogen ist. Jahwes Macht und Herrlichkeit setzt sich nach seinem Willen und Plan in der Welt durch.[11]

This lengthy rehearsal of Fichtner's analysis, though somewhat onesided and schematic, seems warranted within our pursuit, as it points up rather clearly the affinity between the reversal-motif in Isaiah and the properties of the woe-cry discerned in our exegetical survey and summarized in the first section of this chapter.

Fichtner published his article in 1953, without reference to von Rad's basic study of Holy War[12]. The latter makes it possible to anchor the general motif, observed by Fichtner, in Israel's sacred traditions and to understand it theologically. More than any other prophet, Isaiah speaks within the context of a Holy War ideology:

> ... sind es doch gerade die Gedanken, die für besonders zentral und charakteristisch für Jesaja gelten, die dem Propheten von dieser Tradition [der Tradition des Heiligen Krieges] her zugeflossen sind. Von da her hatte er den Glaubensgedanken, von da her die Ablehnung von Rüstung und Bündnissen, von da her das Motiv des Schauens auf Jahwe und des Stillhaltens. Es ist wohl nicht zu viel gesagt, daß Jesaja das gesamte universale Geschichtshandeln Jahwes — den מעשה יהוה — in der Form des heiligen Krieges schaut, eines letzten, also eschatologischen Aufbruchs und Kampfes Jahwes um den Zion.[13]

In his study of the origin of the concept of the Day of Yahweh[14] the "work of Yahweh", understood here in relation to Holy War, is related to the Day of Yahweh[15]. The investigation of Soggin[16] into the function of Holy War as punishment against Israel, sharpens this aspect of the thought complex under discussion, an aspect implicit

---

[9] Ibid. 463.

[10] Ibid.

[11] Ibid. 464.

[12] G. von Rad, Der Heilige Krieg im alten Israel, 1958[3]; first published 1951.

[13] Ibid. 61 f. Von Rad analyzes, among other passages, the Holy War content of the woe-pericopes Is 31 1-5 (59f.) Is 5 12 (59, n. 99) Is 17 12ff. (62) Is 5 12. 19 10 12 (62, n. 107).

[14] Von Rad, The Origin of the Concept of the Day of Yahweh, op. cit.

[15] Von Rad's synthesis is spelled out more fully in his Theologie, II 154—181.

[16] J. A. Soggin, Der prophetische Gedanke über den Heiligen Krieg, als Gericht gegen Israel, op. cit.

in von Rad's basic study[17]. Seen in this light, Fichtner's *Umkehrung* becomes Israel's turn toward the dictates of political and military reason, to the detriment of reliance on Yahweh in the tradition of Holy War. The *Umkehrung* of the punishment, then, becomes the reversion of Yahweh's Holy War against those who, in their *hybris*, abandon trust in Yahweh and attempt to "go it alone". The nations become the instruments of Yahweh, in such a case, but meet the same fate if they, in turn, act in self-styled sovereignty.

Our exegisis has shown how the *hôy*-pericopes in Isaiah not only announce punishment—both against Israel and the nations—in the form of reversal, but tend to do so within the frame of reference of the Holy War-Day of the Lord panorama, a panorama within which the first extant occurrences of *hôy* (Am 5 18 6 1) were already embedded. It is inviting to think that Isaiah took up the use of *hôy* from Amos precisely because of its association with that panorama in Amos and became the prophet to use *hôy* most freqnently because of the prominence in his proclamation of precisely that theme within which *hôy* had, in all probability, found entrance into prophecy.

While the potential of *hôy* to express contrast, reversal from an acceptable life situation to gloom and darkness—a potential brought along from its funerary background—may have been enough to link it to a panorama of theological thought that involves so much of such reversal, we need to ask whether there might not be further ties between reversal, we need to ask whether there might not be further ties between *hôy* and the Holy War-Day of the Lord ideology. More specifically, does the fact that Amos, Micah, and to some extent Isaiah, show awareness of the background of *hôy* in funerary lamentation suggest that *hôy* may have entered the Holy War-Day of the Lord context in its specific capacity as a mourning cry? To test this possibility it is necessary to examine that context, in passages which present it fairly fully but do not involve *hôy*, for the presence of expressions of mourning lamentation.

III. The Mourning Motif Within the Day of Yahweh

A survey of the passages that form the exegetical basis for the concept of the Day of Yahweh[18] reveals the presence of the motif of

---

[17] Von Rad incorporates Soggin's analysis into his picture of Holy War and the Day of the Lord (Theologie II 133). The cosmic dimension provided by the studies of Cross and Miller (see above, 42, n. 6) needs to be added for a fuller panorama, however.

[18] Von Rad (The Origin of the Concept of the Day of Yahweh 97, n. 2) singles out the following: Is 2 12 13 6. 9 22 5 34 8   Jer 46 10   Ez 7 19 13 5 30 3   Joel 1 15 2 1. 11 3 4 4 14   Am 5 18-20   Obad 15   Zeph 1 7. 8. 14-18   Zech 14 1. Černý (The Day of Yahweh,

wailing/mourning in a variety of manifestations. In Is 13 16 we read
the formula: הילילו כי קרוב יום יהוה.

Similarly in Ez 30 2f.[19]: הילילו הה ליום כי קרוב יום.

Several exhortations to mourn (בכו והילילו, verse 5; אלי, verse 8;
הילילו . . . הגרו וספדו verse 13) lead up to the cry of Joel 1 15[20]:
אהה ליום כי קרוב יום יהוה

In Zeph 1 the exhortation הילילו ישבי המכתש (verse 11) is flanked by
the formula (הגדול) קרוב יום יהוה (verses 7. 14)[21]. The announcement
of the Day of Yahweh in Is 22 5 is followed by the accusation (verses 12-13) that there should have been mourning instead of joy:

> In that day the Lord God of hosts
>   called to weeping and mourning,
>   to baldness and girding with sackcloth;
> and behold, joy and gladness,
>   slaying oxen and killing sheep,
>   eating flesh and drinking wine.

In Ez 7 the Day, repeatedly announced as imminent, a day marked
by reversal of fate wrought through the Lord's vengeance, is again
characterized as a day of mourning (verses 18. 27). Finally, the Book of
Lamentations, from a stance *post eventu*, actualizes the mourning
demanded by the breaking in of the Day for Jerusalem.

The pericope Jer 6 1-6, Soggin's paradigm of Holy War directed
against Israel[22], contains the *Schreckruf* אוי לנו (verse 4)[23]. A similar

---

Appendix I) selects basically the same pericopes; he omits Is 22 5 Ez 13 5 and adds
Mal 3 23 (45) Zeph 2 2. 3 Lam 2 22.

[19] The text of this expression is unstable. LXX omits הילילו, but repeats the interjection (ὦ ὦ ...). This repetition may reflect two words expressive of mourning in
the *Vorlage*. Vulgate has both features (Ululate; vae, vae ...). Zimmerli (Ezechiel 724)
wonders whether a second woe-cry could not have been transformed into הילילו
later. Even such an adaptation (or simply, a secondary addition of הילילו) would be
evidence, however, for a tradition associating the elements of the formula with each
other. Perhaps the LXX's doubling simply shows Greek style (cf. Οἴμμοι οἴμμοι
οἴμμοι for אהה, Joel 1 15). The hapax הה is doubtlessly releated to the more frequent אהה (cf. Joel 1 15), as an abbreviation, scribal corruption, or a variant.

[20] Wolff (Dodekapropheton, Joel 22ff.) analyzes carfully the significant place of this
Schreckensruf within its context, characterized as "Die Gattung 'Aufruf zur Volksklage'" (cf. Excursus on that genre, ibid. 23f.).

[21] It is interesting to note that the introductory formula of verse 7 (. . . הס) is also found,
slightly changed, at the conclusion of the *hôy*-series of Hab 2. May we add this as a
further small item of evidence for the association of *hôy* with Yahweh's Day?!

[22] Soggin, Der prophetische Gedanke, 79. Cf. Bach, Die Aufforderungen zur Flucht und
zum Kampf, 18f.

[23] LXX has ὦ πόλις ψευδής in verse 6. This suggests *hôy*. If this could be accepted as
original, as we are inclined to do, we would have here an interesting employment of

context contains the אוי of Jer 4 13. 31. אוי is also spoken over Moab, the victim of Holy War waged against her by the Ammonites (cf. Jer 48 46). It is the cry put into the mouth of the Philistines by the writer of I Sam (4 7.8), who attributes to the situation the character of Holy War, in such a way, however, that the punishment is reverted against Israel.

אהה, noted already in Joel 1 15, can be found in the Holy War context of II Kings 3 10, where it is a lamenting cry in anticipation that the Lord would give the three kings into the hand of Moab. That אהה and אוי can perform similar functions is indicated by the similarity of the situation in Judg 6 22 Jer 1 6 (אהה) and Is 6 5 (אוי).

הילילו, noted in Is 13 16 Ez 30 2 Joel 1 5ff. Zeph 1 11, is the exhortation to Judah and Jerusalem because of the approaching onslaught of the Divine Warrior (Jer 4 8), and very similarly in Jer 25 34 and, with reference to Heshbon, in Jer 49 3 (singular). The destruction announced in Mic 1 leads the prophet to exhort himself (verse 8; cohortative) to anticipatory lamentation. The imperative appears in the somewhat enigmatic Holy War pericope Zech 11 1-3.

This may suffice to establish a rather regular place for anticipatory mourning within the Holy War-Day of the Lord pattern[24]. Our first several examples (Is 13 16 Ez 30 2 Joel 1 15 Zeph 1) show that this feature could gain rather fixed formulaic character. On the other hand, the lack of standardization and the variety of verbal forms and interjections used forbid the isolation of any one specific form for the call to, or expression of mourning in this pattern[25]. Instead, one gains the impression that it was the presence of such a call or expression, rather

---

ʾôy and hôy with reference to the same situation. Those who are threatened by Holy War break out into the Schreckruf ʾôy, while the threat to them is expressed by hôy: We would not emend הפקד to הֻשְׁקַר, on the basis of LXX ψευδής. הפקד is not only lectio difficilior, but also a root frequently associated with hôy. It is better to read: הוי עיר הפקד, "Hôy, city to be punished."

[24] The association of the "Aufruf zur Volksklage" (see above, 88, n. 20) with the Day of the Lord has been recognized also by Wolff (Dodekapropheton, Joel 25). Of הילילו in particular he says: "Eben dieses הילילו ist aber das ständig wiederkehrende Leitwort des bei Joel voraufgehenden Aufrufs zur Klage: [Joel:] 5 (8aG) 11. 13. Es gehört ebenso in Jes 13 6 und Zeph 1 11 (vgl. 14ff.) zur Topik der Ansage des Tages Jahwes. So baut der Klageaufruf in 5-14 großartig den Topos 'Heulet!' in den Tag-Jahwe-Androhungen aus." The place and function of mourning in this context, perhaps related to the cursing of the enemy before a campaign (cf. J. H. Hayes, The Usage of Oracles Against Foreign Nations in Ancient Israel, JBL 87, 1968, 81—92) awaits further study.

[25] That הילילו (and related forms), אהה and אוי stand in other contexts is clear. For a characterization of the former two see Wolff (ibid. 23-25). The latter has been treated by Wanke (see above, 24f.).

than any particular formulation of it, which formed an expected part of the pattern.

As such a call to, or proleptic expression of mourning we assume, did *hôy* make its entry into the proclamation of prophecy, either in Amos or earlier. In time, however—and the marks of this development are clear, though not absolute in Isaiah already—it became specialized to express the foreboding and threatening aspect of that call, a function for which the lament-vengeance range that constitutes its background made it immensely suitable. The specialization continued until the mourning quality of *hôy* had been all but lost, so that the Holy War-Day of the Lord pericopes in the prophets resort to other words to express the call to mourning.

IV. *Hôy* Beyond Isaiah

The remaining Old Testament *hôy*-words bear the marks of standing in a tradition already, rather than of shaping a tradition. By and large, the characteristics of *hôy* in Isaiah[26] are continued. The marks of development observable[27] consist of a lessening consciousness of the funerary background and of increased evidence of bitterness in tone[28].

The *hôy*-words of Jer 22 seem to form an exception to the first trend. It may be, however, as our discussion of that pericope explains[29], that Jeremiah's juxtaposition of *hôy* in its original function of funerary lamentation with *hôy* in its specialized prophetic use must be seen as a conscious re-employment of that original function which had been left behind by the spezialized development. Then Jer 22 would be supportive evidence for the trend just observed, rather than an exception to it. The other Jeremianic woes are in line with that trend.

The woe-oracles of Hab 2 certainly carry a vengeance-thrust, without any evidence of a mourning quality, unless a trace of it be contained in the enigmatic verse 2 11. Traces of association of *hôy* with mourning are present in Zephaniah. In Nahum and in Jer 47. 48. 50—51 *hôy*

---

[26] Summarized above, 61 ff.

[27] We need to remind ourselves that our evidence consists of a handful of extant samples scattered throughout writings from at least 240 years, a basis slim indeed for any attempt to outline a development.

[28] Here we agree in principle with Clifford (The Use of *Hôy* in the Prophets). We hold, however, that this development has its basis in Isaiah's use of *hôy* already, even though the funerary background is still in evidence there, in contrast to Clifford who sees it as a basically exilic and post-exilic development. We have to reject Clifford's syntactical evidence for this development, however. The instances where *hôy* is followed by a preposition have been explained differently (cf. above, 24 ff.).

[29] See above, 71 ff.

stands in units filled with expressions of mourning and lamentation, but it cannot be associated with these in such a way as to demonstrate that it itself functions as one of them. In fact, we may have evidence here to support the observation[30] that other words had to express the mourning characteristically associated with the Holy War-Day of the Lord pattern. The *hôy*-words of Ezekiel, II Isaiah and Zechariah appear to be epigonal in character.

In the understanding of the Septuagint translators[31], *hôy* had become absorbed again into that broad stream of interjections from which it had separated itself for some time to serve a specialized function within a prophetic motif, a function within which it could not establish itself to the point of formulaic distinctness because of the pull exerted upon it by the stream of related interjections flowing along beside it, a pull which it could not resist because it lacked sufficient conceptual, grammatical and phonetic "body" to assert itself. If a metaphorical conclusion be allowed, we have written the story of the heroic but unsuccessful attempt of a brave little interjection to become a big word.

---

[30] See above, 90.
[31] See above, 25.

Walter de Gruyter
Berlin · New York

Beihefte zur Zeitschrift
für die alttestamentliche Wissenschaft
Herausgegeben von Georg Fohrer